ALL FOR HEAVEN, HELL, OR HOBOKEN

APUSH 2022

Congratulations Tomo!

[signature]

My Life in the Army
Inlistment to
the Front
May. 16th to Sept. 27th

May 15 8:30 P. M. Phone from
Dr Robbins

16
Left Bristol at 9:20 P. M.
with Dr. Robbins for Farmington
Draft Board # 2 Hartford County.
Sent to Washington DC. Left
Hartford at 11 A. M. was watching
Ruth, went with me to W.
Arrived N. Y. 2:05 P. M. Left
2:30 reached Washington D. C
at 9:20 P. M. Stayed at Hotel
Harris.

Note Left Wash. DC Jul. 8d
Monday at 9:20 P. M.
I was 4 days at Wash. D.C.

The World War I diary of Private Clair M. Pfennig

ALL FOR HEAVEN, HELL, OR HOBOKEN

The World War I Diary and Letters of
Clair   M. Pfennig, Flash Ranger,
Company D, 29th Engineers, A.E.F.

Edited by
Anthony G. Finan

CRIMSON ☘ SHAMROCK PRESS
Saint Louis, Missouri

this book is dedicated to Debbie, Alex, Alison and Anne

Published by Crimson Shamrock Press
St. Louis, Missouri

Printed in the U.S.A.

"Library of Congress Catalog Card Number:" 98-73496
ISBN 0-9666821-0-6

Cover Design: Jerry McCabe.
Cover Photograph: 29th Engineers reorganized into 1st Battalion, 74th
          Engineers upon their arrival at Fort Stuart, Newport News, VA on
          March 11, 1919
Page ii Diary Photograph: Debra Finan
Maps: Anthony Finan

CONTENTS

MAPS

INTRODUCTION

Clair Merchant Pfennig was born in Bristol, Connecticut on October 25, 1891. He was the son of Frank A. and Anna May (Merchant) Pfennig.

Clair Pfennig attended the local grammar school in Bristol and graduated from Bristol High School in 1910. At the University of Connecticut, then known as the Connecticut Agricultural College, he pursued an Engineering degree in the School of Mechanical Arts. He adapted well to the curriculum which stressed the Sciences, Mathematics, and Applied Engineering; the majority of his college grades were in the A-/B+ range. After two years of study, he qualified for his undergraduate diploma, and he received it on June 18, 1913. He remained at the university for the 1913-14 academic year acting as a student instructor and worked within the university's engineering department as it planned new construction for the expanding campus.

In January, 1915 he took a job with Sperry and Buell, a Bristol engineering company. He worked at the firm until his induction into the service.

At the age of 26, Clair Pfennig was drafted into the National Army of the United States to fight in the World War. After basic training at the Washington D.C. Barracks, he was assigned to Company D, 29th Engineers. On July 9, 1918 Private Pfennig boarded a transport ship in Hoboken, New Jersey bound for Europe.

Upon arrival in France, Private Pfennig travelled by rail to the Lorraine district of France. In August, he attended advanced training school for engineers at Fort St. Menge outside the town of Langres. There he received specialized instruction in flash ranging at the newly-created Flash and Sound Ranging School. Private Pfennig was assigned to Flash Ranging Section #2, 2nd Battalion Flash and Sound Rangers in September. The unit joined the U.S. Second Army and took up position at the front in the Toul sector of the Lorraine, outside the town of Thiaucourt. From this locaton, elements of the Second Army threatened the German garrison city of Metz as the U.S. First Army carried out the Meuse-Argonne Offensive just to the west. Private Pfennig remained on the front line until the Armistice was signed on November 11, 1918.

After the war ended, his unit was one of the few chosen to travel into Luxembourg and Germany as an occupying force. In December, the unit was withdrawn from Germany and ordered home. Following a lengthy bout with influenza, Private Pfennig finally returned to the U.S. on March 11, 1919. He received his honorable discharge 11 days later.

When he returned home to Bristol, Clair Pfennig married Ruth E. Olson, the woman to whom he had proposed prior to his induction. Little is recorded about Ruth Pfennig other than that she was of Swedish descent and had three sisters. She is said to have towered over her husband who was a man of very short and slight stature. The couple was childless.

In 1920, he returned to the engineering firm of Sperry and Buell. At the time, the company did much of the engineering work for the city of Bristol. Carleton W. Buell, the founder of the firm, was also the City Engineer in Bristol. Clair Pfennig became secretary-treasurer of Sperry and Buell and Mr. Buell's assistant. When Mr. Buell died in 1941, Sperry and Buell dissolved as a company. The city council of Bristol hired Clair Pfennig as the city's chief engineer, a position he held for 20 years until his retirement in 1961.

Professionally, Clair Pfennig was a registered engineer and land surveyor in the state of Connecticut. He was a member of the Phi Mu Delta fraternity of the University of Connecticut and the Connecticut Society of Civil Engineers.

Clair Pfennig was very active in the local American Legion Post. He was one of the original members of the Seicheprey Post No. 2. From 1936-37, he was post commander. At the state level he held posts of adjutant and district commander.

A Mason most of his adult life, he belonged to Stephen Terry Lodge 2, Dunbar Encampment. He was also a member of the West Cemetary Association and the Prospect Methodist Church.

At the age of 81, Clair M. Pfennig died on August 22, 1973. He was a patient at the Cheshire Rehabilitation Center. Funeral services were held at the Prospect Methodist Church, and he is buried in the West Cemetary in Bristol, Connecticut.

I discovered Private Pfennig's war diary in the attic of my mother-in-law's home in St. Louis. She had purchased it at an antique shop in Middleton, Connecticut on a mid-'70's trip back to visit relatives. The diary is contained in a bound, three inch by five inch pocketbook of graph paper. It is covered with an olive drab fabric. Inside the diary is a slip from the American Library Association, an organization that distributed thousands of similar battlefield pocket diaries to American troops during the Great War.

The diary itself is less than a traditional narrative; it is more a staccato of observations penciled in by Private Pfennig as he experienced the World War. I have reproduced his manuscript in *italics*, including his artwork, and two letters he wrote home as carefully as possible in order to preserve the inherent roughness of his chronicle. Misspellings on his part, whether they are in English or French, have been left intact. I have added corrections only to clarify the names of persons and places. The explanatory passages , maps, and National Archives photographs are intended to provide historical perspective and background to the events of Private Pfennig's military career.   AGF

STRANGE EXPLOIT OF
SCIENCE IN BATTLES

Veteran Engineer Tells how
Germany's Big Guns
Were Silenced

Members of the 74th Engineers yesterday lifted the veil of secrecy which has shrouded that flash and sound organization, unfolding a tale of scientific exploits on the battlefield which almost reads like a Jules Verne story.

The flash and sound organization located enemy guns on the west front by timing the flash of the gun and the roar as the shell left the weapon. Its operations were secret and this is the first time that the men have been allowed to even mention to what organization they belonged.

Microphones were set up all along the front lines. These sound detection machines were linked to a central station further in the rear. The detectors recorded sounds to the hundredth part of a second and with them the American artillery was enabled to locate hidden German batteries and score direct hits.

The organization just out of a training camp in France was stationed in Toul sector where the Germans started the great drive which was the beginning of their defeat. Members of the unit say the Boche had superiority of the air and that American and Allied planes and balloons were unable to go up and locate many batteries.

On information furnished by the flash and sound unit American artillery laid down its first barrage, a feat that went down in history as one of the most perfectly executed of the war.

The flash unit of the organization went with the infantry all through the Chateau Thierry drive, locating enemy guns by calculating the time the sound was heard, the time it was seen and the speed with which sound, light, and projectiles travel. The men were cited by the Major General commanding the Americans in that sector for their dedicated work.

The 74th went all the way way from Chateau Thierry to Ponta Mousson. The unit was organized at Fort de St. Menge in January 1918. Company B, Twenty-ninth Engineers had been designated for this work, and forty men of the 116th Engineers were taken as a nucleus for the organization.

In France the outfit was known as Second Battalion, Twenty-ninth Engineers. They were dubbed the 74th a short time before they left France in order that they might be sent home, some rule conflicting with their departure it is understood. The First Battalion, Twenty-ninth, a map making unit, still is in France.

Men in the 74th think the world of all of their officers and there is not one of them who would not go throu fire and water for them, especially Major Theodore Lyman. The major was professor of science at Princeton University before going to war.

Captain C.B. Bazzoni, known among his men as the sound ranging Wizard also is a scientist. He was in England on research for the Smithsonian Institute when he entered the service.

The men in the outfit were selected for their mathematical ability, sound judgement, and all around good qualities.

The Newport News Daily Press, Newport News, Virginia,
March 13, 1919

Departure from Bristol--Enlistment--Washington D.C.--
Washington Barracks--Medical Examinations
MAY 1918

America's most famous recruiting poster

My Life in the Army

Inlistment to

the Front

May, 16<u>th</u> to Sept. 27th

May 15 8:30 P.M. Phone from Dr. Robbins

16

Left Bristol at 9:20 P.M. with Dr. Robbins for Farmington Draft Board #2 Hartford County.

Sent to Washington D.C. Left Hartford at 11 A.M. via Waterbury Ruth went with me to W. Arrived N.Y. 2:05 P.M. left 2:3 Penn Sta. reached D.C. Hotel Harris.

*Note Left Wash. DC July 8th Monday at 9:20 P.M.
7 Wks 4 Days at Wash. D.C.*

On April 6, 1917, Woodrow Wilson and the Congress of the United States officially committed the country to "the Great Crusade" in Europe. Of immediate concern to President Wilson and his advisors was the creation of a credible fighting force that could be deployed across the Atlantic. The exact composition of this army was a point of contention early on. Some called for a predominately volunteer force based on Civil War and Spanish-American War models. Former President Theodore Roosevelt was a staunch advocate of this position. He even approached President Wilson with the idea of leading a volunteer division himself, "Rough-rider style." Others favored a conscripted army. General John J. Pershing, the designated Commander of the American Expeditionary Force (A.E.F.), and a majority of Army staff officers were outspoken critics of the volunteer system.

General Pershing's support of selective service was based on both military practicality and political symbolism. According to General Pershing, the evils of the volunteer system were readily apparent in past history. Abuses that occurred during the Civil War included the appointment of ill-prepared politicians to high command positions and the conferrence of Medals of Honor to entire regiments based on dubious distinction. From a practical standpoint, the Union's volunteer system did not produce the steady number of troops needed to subdue the South. Eventually, President Abraham Lincoln signed into law a Selective Service Act in 1863 to raise the necessary number of men. General Pershing also believed a vote for conscription would send an important message of American resolve to friend and foe alike. Said General Pershing,

> . . . Universal service is the only principle to follow that will lead to success in this war, and that should be well understood. We are in this thing for keeps and it is going to demand the utmost exertion and the preparation to win. We shall have to select the flower of the young manhood of this country and give them thorough training before we start.

Upon passage of the Selective Service Act of 1917, General Pershing commented on its significance,

> The echo of that vote for conscription will be heard around the globe. It is a triumph of democratic government; a willing step taken by free people under wise leadership. It means that every man will have his role to play. To have a hand in affairs and know that he is part of the system will make a better citizen of every man.

The Draft Act required every man between the ages of 21 and 31 to register for military service. Close to 10 million men signed on to Selective Service rolls. For the first wave of selection on July 20, 1917, each man was given a number between 1 and 10,500. Blindfolded officials chose enough numbers to yield a 687,000 man army. Eventually, over 24 million men between the ages of 18 and 45 registered with Selective Service. Clair M. Pfennig was one of the 3 million called into active military service.(1)

May 17th
Left for Wash. Barracks Penn. Ave. car transferred to 4 1/2 St. car. Reported Sergent Major. Sent to Hospital on call 322 after some red tape. Sent to Co. D 29th Eng. Went to hospital 2:30 sent back to company. Filled straw mattress got misc. equipment eat mess and turned in for night. Captain Messer on liquor question

Wash. Bks; Eng army post regular and replacement C.O. Back Brig. Gen.-U.S. War College situated at extreme end of parade ground.

Captain Thomas H. Messer was an officer of the 29th Engineers. The "liquor question" no doubt referred to General Pershing's concern over the easy availability of alcoholic beverages in France. In his memoirs, General Pershing commented:

> My most earnest thought and attention were given to this subject early in our experience and throughout the war. The habit of drinking was not only detrimental to efficiency but led to other indiscretions. It is a question whether under ordinary circumstances in times of peace a healthy moral sentiment cannot be created as a safeguard against excesses, yet during the war when men were not surrounded by the restraining influences of home life limited prohibition was necessary.

In January of 1918, Pershing issued a memorandum on the subject to all officers of the A. E. F. It specifically forbade American soldiers from purchasing or receiving as gifts whiskey, brandy, champagne, liquors, or other alcoholic beverages other than light wines and beer.(2)

The Commanding Officer of the Corps of Engineers was Brigadier General William M. Black. Although engineer soldiers participated in the early stages of the Revolutionary War, a Corps of Engineers was not officially created by the Continental Congress until March 11, 1779. This first Corps of Engineers was disbanded in November 1783. Congress sanctioned a new Corps of Artillerists and Engineers on May 9, 1794. A distinction was made between these two departments on March 16, 1802 when Congress authorized a separate Corps of Engineers. From 1818 onward, the Office of the Chief of Engineers was based in Washington, D.C. The Washington Barracks was one of five national training centers for enlisted men entering Regular Army engineer units.(3)

> *May 18th*
> > *Went up for exam at 9 A.M. and 1 P.M. written up and Rush Exam finished at 5 P.M. with finger prints*
> > > *1st Inoculation and vacination*
> > > *With a return card for two more*

> *May 20th*
> > *Started life of a soldier*

> *May 27*   *2nd Inoculation*
> > *2nd Vacination*
> > *280 in Company*
> *80% College men every state represented but five.*

Inspection--Unit Formed--Training

JUNE 1918

> **June 1**
> > **First Inspection**
>
> **Made out**
> > **Insurance   10,000**
> > > **Payable-   Mrs. A. M. P f-**
> > > **Mr. F. A. P f**
>
> **beginning June 1st 1918**
> **Premium   6.20 per month**
>
> **Made Allotment   15.00   Cancealed**
> > **beginning June 1st- Mr. F. A. P. f- July 1st**

American servicemen took out 19 billion dollars of life insurance during the course of World War I. In a note of appreciation to Secretary of the Treasury William G. McAdoo, General Pershing remarked:

> All ranks of the A.E.F. appreciate deeply the generous measures the government has taken to provide insurance for their families, in proof of which more than 90 per cent of the men have taken insurance. This wise provision for their loved ones heartens our men and strengthens the bonds that unite the army and people in our strong determination to triumph in our most righteous cause. (1)

The initials above referred to Private Pfennig's parents. Frank A. Pfennig and the former Anna May Merchant were married on September 11, 1888 at the residence of the bride's parents. The Bristol Press described the ceremony as "one of the prettiest home weddings that has ever taken place in Bristol."(2)

> **June 6th**
> > **3d Innoculation**
> > **Vacinations given up but Innoc. very effective.**

>   ***Officers in charge***
>   ***Capt. Messer***
>   ***Capt. Younge***
>   ***Lieut. Leui*** [Leue] ***(Shit)***

Officers of the 29th Engineers:
>   Captain George B. Younge
>   Second Lieutenant Conrad F. Leue, Washington,
>   D.C.

>   ***June 7th***   ***CoD 29th Eng***
>   ***to Co F 603 Eng.***   ***Capt. Messer***
>   ***Capt Younge-Co D 29th to Co F 604th***

Company D, 29th Engineers was designated Company F, 603rd Engineers until the unit departed for France on July 8, 1918. It then reverted back to its old designation, Company D, 29th Engineers. A Company E, 29th Engineers was organized at Camp Devens, Massachusetts on March 29, 1918. It was sent to the Washington Barracks on May 27. This company became Company F, 604th Engineers on June 6. It left for France on August 14. Upon arrival on September 5, it also regained its earlier title Company E, 29th Engineers.(3)

>   ***June 10th***
>   ***First Hike***

>   ***16th***
>   ***Went to city and Marshal Hall - Hot Day***

>   ***28th***
>   ***Hike light pack Potomac Park 10 miles***

>   ***21th Inspection by Major McCumber with full pack.***

23d *Went throu Congressional Library-John Cabin
Md.
Trolley caugh fire*

24th *Hike and inspection whole battalion 1200-603d
Eng Ready for over sea duty and full equipment*

Sightseeing in D.C.--Unit readied for overseas--Parade past Capital--Departure by train for New York--Officers in Command--Summary of days at sea--Arrival at Hoboken-- Departure on USS Toloa--Convoy joined--Daily Schedule-- U-Boat alert--Landing at Brest--Camp at Napoleon's Prison-- "A rough sea"--Boarding the "French Pullman"--Rennes-- Tours--Bourges--Dijon--Camp Williams--Arrival at Langres Station--Trucked to Longeau--The village

JULY 1918

July 1918

July 4th
Went throu Nat Museum and Zoo park. Saw Parade at Penn Ave and Pageant at Capital.

The Fourth of July Pageant held in Washington, D.C. was vividly recounted in the *Washington Post* on the following day:

> What will go down in history as one of the most impressive, dramatic, and inspiring demonstrations of the period of the world-war was staged on the cast front of the Capitol last night, when the climax of the greatest of all independence day celebrations was achieved in the presentation of the pageant 'Democracy Triumphant.'
>
> While the pageant itself was picturesque, colorful, and inspiring, a far greater dramatic effect was created by the setting, the surroundings, and the tens of thousands of spectators among whom were representatives of all the nations fighting against German autocracy, as well as of those oppressed peoples now seeking to throw off the German yoke.
>
> Following presentation during the afternoon of a series of picturesque tableaux representing all the allied nations, on and in the vicinity of the White House Ellipse, the participants formed in a great parade and marched down Pennsylvania avenue to the Capitol where they were reviewed by the President and Mrs. Wilson and attaches of all the embassies and legations of foreign governments now represented here.
>
> The parade, which was led by the Serbian unit, was made up according to the date of entry of the various nations into the war, and was undoubtedly the most picturesque and colorful pageant ever witnessed in the National Capital. Both sides of Pennsylvania avenue fromTwelfth street to Peace monument were lined with thousands of spectators, who cheered and waved flags as the procession passed.(1)

July 6th Ordered send dress suite cases home

July 7th

Passes restricted from 10 A.M.-2 P.M. +
2 P.M.-8 P. M.

Received rest of equipment
Saw St. Louis vs Washington 3-2 score
Weight 132 lbs

"SOTHORON HOLDS NATIONALS AS BROWN-IES HIT JOHNSON" headlined the July 8 column of Washington Post sportswriter J.V. Fitzgerald. In this American League contest, St. Louis Browns pitcher Allan Sothoron blanked the Washington Nationals on three hits. According to Fitzgerald, Sothoron's pitching was dazzling. Throughout the contest, Washington batters swung at "large chunks of ozone." It was as if Sothoron just plain "chloroformed" them. Surprisingly, the Nationals' ace pitcher Walter Johnson took the loss. He was touched for eight hits including two by Brownie slugger George Sisler. To add insult to injury, "aged and agile Jimmy Austin stole home in the ninth while Walter was winding up and perhaps making mind bets with himself on his chances of taking the Browns into camp before the campaign ends." Prior to the game, Nationals manager Clark Griffith donated five hundred baseballs "for the soldier guests of the club to scramble for and the boys in khaki swarmed over the field as if they were on a Hun hunt."(2)

July 8 Departed for Over Sea

Passes none. Packs made ready for shipment
bags packed 8 A.M. Whole Battallion 603d Eng 750 and staff
Inspected at 2 P.M. Retreat at 5:30 P.M. Mess 5:40 Passed
review at 6:30 by Post Commander
8:00 P.M. boarded train Delaware and Hudson
Past review at Capital lead by band.
9:20 P.M. pulled out of Wash. Train #2 Car 12
Not much sleep. Phil on B+O o N.Y. on Reading. Four
trains 14 cars each left Wash
Bag again shiped near Phil.

9:20 A.M.-9:20 P.M.-9:20 P.M.
7 wks + days in Washington D.C.

Officers Command of Boat

AF Troops
          Col. Rogers U.S.A
(killed on Am Front Sept 6 1918)
          Command 603d Eng
                    Major McCumber
                    Adj. Geo B. Younge
Co. F 603d
          Capt.   Messer
          Lieut. Leui [Leue]
                    Morrow   *Huston* [Houston]
                    Meade   *Holmes*
                    Kuster [Koester]   *Mea* [May]
          Mascot Browny Co. E.

Officers of the 29th Engineers:
          First Lieutenant Samuel R. Morrow, Carthage,
                    Missouri
          First Lieutenant Fred K. Houston, Beaver,
                    Pennsylvania
          First Lieutenant Clarence F. Holmes, Spokane,
                    Washington
          Second Lieutenant Fred A. Koester, Oakland,
                    California
          Second Lieutenant Louis A. May, Columbia,
                    South Carolina

Summary of Days out etc.
July   9th   Boarded Boat-Toloa
          10th   5:30 P.M. Past Sandy Hook
          11   Thurs.
          12   Climax of War

13

14   **Sunday**

15

16

17

18

19   **Friday-Oversea Convoy**

20

21   **Sunday-Landed 4 P.M.**

22

23

24

Boats known

Yale-Harvard-Mt. Vernon-English Converted Cruiser-Lake Boats

[Editor's Note: This entry appears to have been written in at a chronologically later date.]

The U.S. Troopship Toloa

July 9th

> *Reached N.Y. at 8:00 boarded ferry for Hobokin Examined on board. Landed at U.S. Transport Service Pier #4 at 10:15 Red Cross furnished coffee buns cigaretts and post cards. Boarded Toloa (Cunard) at 11:30 Assigned deck B-15. Soldiers every where. Eight big transports adv 8000 each pulled out at 7:30*

> *Read homework for night a sightly sight-five aparting transports*

Sailed

New York and Newport News Virginia were the two Primary Ports of Embarkation and Debarkation for the United States during World War I. The port facilities for New York were located at Hoboken, New Jersey. To speed the shipment of troops overseas, the Port of New York utilized a number of subports. They included Boston; Philadelphia; Baltimore; Portland, Maine; Halifax, Novia Scotia; St. Johns, Newfoundland; Montreal and Quebec, Canada. The Hoboken facility contained 12 piers, seven warehouses, and an Embarkation Hospital. During the First World War, 1,777,109 troops passed through the Primary Port of Embarkation, Hoboken and its subports. Of these, 699,713 left from Hoboken itself.(3)

The *Toloa* was a United Fruit Company banana boat which had been converted into a World War I troopship. The ship carried 2,390 troops to France on its two crossings of the Atlantic.(4)

July 10th

> *Revealry 6:00*
> *Mess 7:00*
> *Land time changed to ship time 1:00 to 12:00*
> *12:00 Moore pulled off pier and drift out.*
> *1:30 Droped anchor alon side three others. Prettily Camoflaged-Yellow dragon*
> *5:00 Pulled Anchor*

5:20 Past Sandy Hook outer light
6:30 Thunderstorm struck wireless
8:00 U.S.Destroyers joined. Turned in. Water rough.
8:30 lights out

Three transports; 2 destroyers; 1 battleship

A dragon at sea--an American ship painted with "dazzle" camouflage

Since the naval segment of World War I was fought without the benefit of radar and sonar technology, a high premium was still put on seeing the enemy with human eyes. Vice Admiral Albert Gleaves, U.S.N., Commander of Convoy Operations in the Atlantic, elaborated on the use of camouflage by ships to combat the effectiveness of German U-Boat Captains:

> Wide use was made of camouflage painting of hulls and exterior fittings of all types of ships, to confuse the enemy in estimating the course, speed and size of his quarry.
>
> For a long time, it was generally thought that camouflage acted like the invisible cloak of the knight in the fairy tale, which of course it didn't.
>
> There were various styles of camouflage just as there were different kinds of zigzag. Some camouflage was so effective that the course of the ship was disguised as much as 90 degrees. Once an officer of the deck reported that a ship had been sighted heading directly across his bow, when as a matter of fact she was going in the same direction.

> Any one living in New York City during the war had opportunity to see from Riverside Drive the various designs of camouflage. Some of these were fantastic but the majority were known as the 'dazzle system,' which sufficiently indicates the style.

The "dazzle system" to which the Vice Admiral refers involved painting on the the ships irregular, geometric patches of color. The colors included blues, grays, greens, and even yellows. Against the backdrop of the ocean, it is very difficult for the human eye to distinguish the shape of a vessel when it is painted in such a manner. The bold geometric forms overload the eye's sensory capacity. In effect, the camouflage pattern so 'dazzles" an onlooker that the ship blends in with the surrounding ocean.

Private Pfennig's description of a ship as a "Yellow dragon" is an understandable one. The triangular shapes painted on many Allied vessels resembled the large teeth of a dragon.(5)

Sandy Hook, New Jersey was the home of a U.S. Coast Guard Station.

Allied convoys darkened ships at night as a protective measure. Vice Admiral Gleaves commented, "It was not an easy task to make thousands of men who had never seen a ship before, realize they could neither smoke after sundown or even carry matches. It is a fact that a light of a cigarette may be seen for a half mile, an ample radius for exact submarine torpedo practice, hence the importance of absolute darkness."(6)

> *1st Day Out 1st Day*
> *July 11th*
> > *Reveary*   *@6:00*
> > *Mess*   *6:30*
> *Didn't eat lay around alday*
> > *Medical Inspection*   *3:00*
> > *Turned in*   *8:00*
> > *Lights out*   *8:30*

2nd Day
July 12th
    Revelary   *@6:00*
    Mess   *6:30*
Same old story-Fish
    Joined by five transports total of 11 on trip at
night
    Stormy all day but cleared at night
    Start of Climax of War on Marne at Cheatau Thierry
[Chateau-Thierry] *U.S. Marines-2nd Eng's*

On May 27, the Germans executed their major offensive of 1918. The Aisne Offensive, the brainchild of General Erich Ludendorff, began with the German Seventh Army engaging the French Sixth Army along the Chemin des Dames. The French forces were quickly overwhelmed. Successive defensive positions along the Aisne River and the Vesle River were lost on the first day of fighting. The Germans continued to press the French southward for the next four days. The French retreat left vulnerable a crucial road that connected Chateau-Thierry with Vaux, Meaux and ultimately, Paris, a mere 50 miles to the southwest. Alarmed at this turn of events, General Henri P. Petain, commander of French forces in the field, requested that American troops be moved into the breach as quickly as possible. General Pershing complied, and elements of the 3rd Division engaged German troops within Chateau-Thierry on May 31. The 3rd Division withdrew across the Marne River on June 1 and prohibited a German beachhead from being established on the southern bank. It was here the 3rd Division earned its nickname "The Marne Division."

Stymied at Chateau-Thierry, the German Seventh Army shifted its advance along the Marne towards Vaux and into Belleau Wood, an old hunting preserve. The Americans countered this force with the 2nd Division on June 4. After four weeks of intense combat, the 4th Marine Brigade, the 2nd Engineers, and other elements of the 2nd Division successfully extricated German forces from Belleau Wood. The 2nd Division paid a high price for the victory: 9,777 total casualties, 1,811 deaths. The Germans paid a higher price in defeat, the decimation of four divisions. The 4th Marine Brigade received particular praise for its efforts in the forest. The commmander of the French Sixth Army was so impressed with the infantry brigade that he proposed renaming the wooded area *"Bois de la Brigade de Marne,"* the Wood of the Brigade of the Marne.

Although the momentum of the Aisne Offensive had been effectively halted, the Germans now possessed a salient which they could exploit at a later date. The date would be sooner rather than later. On July 15, German artillery rang out along the Chateau-Thierry front. The *Friedensturm*, or Peace Offensive, had begun. The German plan called for the Seventh Army, which included 11 divisions in the line, four in support, and five in reserve, to attack in a southeastward motion along the Marne near Chateau-Thierry. After capturing the crossing at Epernay and the hills southeast of Reims, the Seventh Army would link up with the 11 divisions of the First Army attacking through the Champagne east of Reims. From there, the advance on Paris could continue.

The American divisions that successfully bore the brunt of the attack in the Marne area were the 42nd, the 28th, and the 3rd. The German armies never fully achieved their objectives. Although the Seventh Army managed to move 10 divisions across the Marne, the First Army was stymied in the Champagne. The offensive ground to a halt. Allied Supreme Commander Marshal Ferdinand Foch sensed this and sought to take advantage of the overextended German armies. On July 18, the Allies counterattacked with a vengeance. The French Tenth Army supplemented by the American 1st and 2nd Divisions pierced the Marne salient below Soissons. The 26th Division advanced from Belleau. Two days later, the 3rd Division crossed the Marne. With Chateau-Thierry all but cut off, the Germans quickly evacuated it. The Allies continued their counteroffensive through the first week of August and eventually reestablished the front on the Aisne. (7)

3d Day

July 13th
    3:00 A.M. Sighted U. Boat
Gun crew at post.
      6:00   Revealry
      6:30   Breakfast
      11:00 Physical Exercise
      2:00   Inspection
      3:00   Medical Exam
Was a fine day, clear. Felt some better after dinner.
11 transports and convoy in party. Cruiser Seatle in lead.

The U.S.S. Seattle

    Toloa in command of U.S. Navy-Captain-right gunners:Boat under English Flags-two others under French rest Amer.
    Time changes every day about 20 minutes
    Saw flying fish on all sides and plenty of porpises, small shark lay on port side!
    Boat drill at 4:00 daily.

Joined by 3 Transports + one destroyer from New Port News

Transports	**11**
Convoy	**3 Destroyers**
	1 Cruiser

When the war broke out with Germany and Austria in 1914, the Atlantic Ocean became the vital lifeline for the European Allies. Both France and Great Britain depended on shipments from the United States to sustain their economies and to supply their war efforts. When the U.S. officially entered the war in April of 1917, the sea routes over which American troops and war material would cross the Atlantic were far from secure. German U-boats prowling the ocean wrought absolute havoc on Allied shipping. Although there were never more than 136 of these vessels operating at sea at any one time, the damage they caused was extensive. Of the ships leaving British ports in the month of April alone, 25 percent never returned. The Allies lost nearly 900,000 tons of cargo space in a span of 30 days. At that point, Allied prospects of winning the war at sea looked about as bleak as those of winning the war on the land.

Allied fortunes in the Atlantic dramatically improved, however, during the summer months of 1917. The introduction of 36 additional American destroyers and the universal adoption of the convoy system limited the effectiveness of the German U-boats considerably. Of the 10,000 ships operating in and out of British posts during the month of August, only one percent was lost. The tide was turning in favor of the Allies in the Atlantic.

German U-boats, although still dangerous, were more of a nuisance than an actual threat to U.S. naval vessels in the summer of 1918. Official reports give credence to only 26 actual contacts between enemy submarines and American ships of the transport force. Seven of these contacts resulted in an American ship being sunk. Although there were undoubtedly more U-boat attacks that went undetected, there were also countless false sightings of torpedo wakes and periscopes. Vice Admiral Albert

Gleaves cited a Captain who "remarked that on the first voyage made by his ship, judging from the periscopes sighted by the lookouts, there must have been a picket fence of submarines stretched across the Atlantic."(8)

The man credited with securing the adoption of the convoy system for Atlantic transport was Rear Admiral William S. Sims. In March of 1917, President Wison dispatched Admiral Sims to England to act as a U.S. liason with the British Admiralty. Admiral Sims was alarmed at the losses sustained by the British in the Atlantic. He proposed grouping ships in convoys for the trip across the ocean. High-ranking British admirals initially scoffed at the idea. They claimed that ships steaming slowly together would provide more of a target than ships steaming singly at top speed. Furthermore, the admirals argued it would take some 25,000 destroyers to effectively patrol the 25,000 square miles of the Atlantic for the slow-moving convoys.

Admiral Sims disputed the admiralty's assertions. He contended that the existing British Grand Fleet was indeed a convoy of sorts protected by destroyer escort and that matching destroyers with convoy fleets at strategic points in the Atlantic would achieve a higher degree of protection than randomly patrolling the entire ocean as was presently the case. In spite of these arguments, the British Admiralty was unmoved. Ultimately, Admiral Sims' idea did manage to reach the ear of a desparate British Prime Minister David Lloyd George. He forced the admiralty to consent to a trial convoy run in early May. It turned out to be a stunning success. The first convoy reached Great Britain on May 20 without the loss of a single ship. On the very next day, the British Admiralty selected a board to implement a convoy system.(9)

The *U.S.S. Seattle* was an armored cruiser. It had the distinction of being the flagship for the first American expeditionary convoy to France in 1917. Under the command of Rear Admiral Albert Gleaves, 14 vessels carried elements of the 1st

Division, about 14,500 troops, to port at St. Nazaire, France.(10)

Because the U.S. possessed a small, deep-sea Merchant Marine Fleet at this time, other Allied nations were required to provide sealift capability for American forces. British steamers carried 48.25 percent of the American Army to Europe. French and Italian vessels transported 2.5 percent and 3 percent respectively. U.S. ships brought over the remaining 46.25 percent of the troops.(11)

The abandon ship drill was a daily event on all troop ships. Soldiers sarcastically referred to it as the "drowning drill."(12)

Convoys containing troop transports were always heavily guarded. A typical escort consisted of a cruiser and two destroyers. Although some destroyers were capable of transatlantic escort duty, thanks to the stationing of refueling tankers in mid-ocean, most escort service involved American-based destroyers passing the convoys off to destroyers out of Queenstown, Ireland at specific rendezvous points in the Atlantic. The U.S. Navy provided 82.75 percent of the escort service across the Atlantic.(13)

4th Day
July 14th Sunday Boat Schedule

6:00	*A.M.*	*Revealry*
6:30		*Mess*
11:00		*Medical Exam*
11:30		*Compulsary Bath*
12:00		*Mess*
4:00		*Boat Drill*
5:30		*Retreat*
7:00		*Turned in Lights Out*
8:30		*All in Closed*

Was pleasant day light sea, had time to rest. One Destroyer left. Joined by one more transport and English converted cruiser. Passed some wreckage around noon. Felt good most of day. Saw school of sharks on star board side.

Run for day a little S.E.

Fleet at Sun Set

Cruiser Seattle U.S.

2   Torpedo Destroyer U.S.

Eng. Converted Cruiser

12   Transports

16

Mt. Vernon (Kronprinzessin Cecile) in convoy-torpedoed Sept 9th 1918 [Editor's Note: This part of the entry seems to have been written in at a later date.]

The U.S. troopship Mount Vernon

Vice Admiral Gleaves devoted an entire chapter of his book to the exploits of the *Mount Vernon*:

The Mount Vernon was formerly the large German passenger ship steamer Kronprinzessin Cecile, gross tonnage 19,503. This ship will be recalled as the 'Gold Ship,' which, in the Summer of 1914, just before the outbreak of the war, sailed from the United States for Germany with a large consignment of gold. While at sea she received notification of Great Britain's war declaration and, being beset with British cruisers, she turned back, affecting her escape by taking advantage of a fog to slip into the small port of Bar Harbor, Maine, where she was interned. Later she was removed under United States Naval Guard to Boston, and upon our entry into the war was fitted out as an American transport.(14)

5th Day

July 15

Same routine during day

3:00 P.M.   Medical Inspection

4:00   Boat Drill

S.O.S called from Norwegean ship. U.S. destroyer responded located sub and returned

Rain-bow in early morning and it meant sailors take morning. Some Sea Sick. Yes sea sick. Water came over front deck.

U-Boat made us a visit-Crosses all changed Depth bombs droped and off in the dark we went.

Vice Admiral Gleaves commented on the use of depth charges:

> Depth bombs, variously known as depth charges or water bombs, were dropped over the stern of a ship, or thrown in pairs, simultaneously to a distance on either side of the vessel by means of a 'Y' gun.
>
> These bombs were fitted with a hydrostatic valve, operated by the weight of the water, so that the charge--300 to 600 pounds of TNT--exploded at a certain depth. If not near enough to blow in the U-boats sides, or to disarrange the delicate internal machinery and fittings, at least it damaged the morale of the crew. (15)

6th Day

July 16th

Same Routine

Was rough all day. No one felt good.

No excitement. Destroyers Left. U.S. Seattle still in command.

Allied vessels in convoy formation

7th Day

July 17th
> *Same Routine*
> *2:30 Gun inspections.*
> *Sea was rough.*
> *Passed into Sub-Zone in early morning. Sub Guard inspected at 5 P.M. Sighted fishing snake off of Port Side.*
> *Ships took zone formation in line Joined by 3 Destroyers*

The "Sub-Zone" mentioned was most likely near the Latitude 48 degrees N and Longitude 25 degrees 50'W. German submarines frequently sailed in this belt enroute from a secret base in the Azores to the British Islands. Convoys took extra care when moving through this zone. Ships frequently employed zigzag tactics within the Sub-Zone to confuse submarine commanders, and troop transports were usually routed through the area in darkness.(16)

8th Day

July 18th
> *Same Routine*
> *Sub-Guard Strong*

Boat Drill at 6 A.M.
Sea calmed down (15)Transports-Convoy(4)
9th Day   July 19th
6:00 A.M.   Revelary
6:30   Mess
7:10   Am. Eng. Fr. Convoy sighted coming all
sides
7:30   U.S. Cruiser Seattle turned back. New
convoy took command (12)
Reported find of Subs loose and convoys active
Inspection of guns and packs, medical inspection and
bunk inspection. Rained off and on during day and put in at
night. Was cool and damp. Saw "Fatherland" Leviathan on
Port Side.

The U.S. troopship Leviathan

Upon America's entry into the war, U.S. Customs officials seized all German ships in U.S. ports. The largest 17 vessels were converted into troop transports. Ships such as the
Frederich der Grosse, the *Kaiser Wilhelm II*, and the *Prinzess
Irene* were renamed the *Huron*, *Agamemnon*, and the *Pocahontas*
respectively. Perhaps the most famous of the impounded German ships was the *Vaterland*. Renamed the *Leviathan*, this vessel was the largest ship in the world. The *Leviathan* could carry
over 9,000 troops at a speed of 23 knots. It transported 48,629
American soldiers to France, more than any other vessel during
the war.(17)

10th Day

July 20
Seven more convoys seen coming in over the
hill.
Transports exchanged and at night with
transports
    15 transports
    14 Convoys
    1 Observation balloon

The exact composition of particular convoys varied. Typically, only 15 percent of the vessels within the Atlantic convoys carried troops. These troop transports were usually routed in special lanes under heavy destroyer escort apart from the cargo convoys. This greatly increased the safety of the troop transports. The overall size of the convoys ranged from 25 to 46 ships.(18)

11th Day

July 21st   *Landed*
5:20 A.M. Past Eng Channel Light- for Breste
[Brest]
5:40 Sighted land which was welcomed sight
6:40 Droped Anchor in harbor and prepared
Y.M.C.A. service at 11:30 A.M. 3:00 P.M. prepared to leave on troop transport. Road on detail to Pa Barracks. Napolean Prison Camp. Sent to field #612 pitched shelter tents at 8:00 P.M. Had supper at 11:20 of roast beef hash and jam and had good night.

Private Pfennig was one of 306,302 American soldiers to land in France in July of 1918. More troops arrived in this month than in any other of the entire war. There were 1,312,208 U.S. soldiers on European soil at this time.(19)

The French port of Brest was the headquarters of Base Section No. 5 for the A.E.F. This coastal city was the leading

port of debarkation for American troops during World War I. With
its four large berths, Brest was capable of handling 42,000 arriving troops in a single day.(20)

American troops arriving in France

The Y.M.C.A. canteen and money exchange in Brest

The French infantry barracks at Pontanezen were used to
house incoming troops. Over a hundred years before, Napoleon
I trained his troops there for an invasion of Britain.(21)

July 22 Monday.
Cool and showers good food. Woke up in the
morning to find our self in a barn yard. French village all of

stone, people used U.S. money. Prices high-but not considering conditions.

   Got some French money need a pocket to carry it. Was camped in mud hole.

   Rained all night
   Two-U-Boats sent out to get Leviathan came in
   Weighed 113 lbs.

Billeting in such areas was quite common. On housing newly-arrived troops, General Pershing wrote:

> It would have been out of the question to supply barracks or tentage for all our troops in France and we adopted the billeting system, whereby troops of a division as they arrived in their training area were spread around by regiments, battalions or companies in the various towns and villages . . .Where there was not enough spare room in the dwelling houses of the inhabitants, which was usually the case, the barn or stable lofts were quickly converted into fairly comfortable quarters, with hay or fodder in lieu of barrack beds or cots. (22)

July 23d
   Cleared at night Battalion moved from our quarters to a grass field.
   Went on guard at 6:30 P.M. Clear night.

July 24th
   Cleared in A.M. Showers throu out day. Little exercise Went on hike around town-Saw observation Balloon hangars. Ordered to be ready to move receive at 3:30 P.M.
   Mid-night supper.

   A rough Sea
     A negro drop to his
   knees and cried aloud:-
     O Lord call this Sea to attention.

My trip over land on
the "French Pullman"

to second rest camp at Longue [Longeau]

July 25

   Bugle sounded at   *1 A.M.*
   Reached R.R. Station 4 A.M.
   Boarded trains at 5:30 A.M.
   Pulled out at   *6:00 A.M.*

   Boarded the "French Pullman" other words
"French Freight Cars" sign on door said 8 Chevaux (about
1/2 the Am. Car Size) 40 Hommes so 42 of us piled. Had a
slow day. Stoped once for coffee. Food issue was good. Slept
on floor. Passed Rennes late at night
   Was hell of trick on the 603d Eng with high
personal

The "Frenchman's Pullman"

  Troops were transported from the port areas to northeastern France by rail. The freight cars used were supposedly capable of carrying eight horses or 40 men comfortably. These figures were even painted onto the sides of most of the cars.

In reality, this mode of transportation was hardly pleasant for American troops moving to the front. While it took 25 to 30 trains to transport one French division, twice as many were required to move one American division. This was due to the fact that the size of a typical American division was approximately twice that of a French division. Critical shortages of rolling stock caused uncomfortable overcrowding on American trains bound for the front in 1918. Thus, most American soldiers did not soon forget their trip on the "French Pullmans." One soldier, Private John O'Brien, 12th Field Artillery, 2nd Division, referred to the "40 and 8's" as transportation designed by the devil. (23)

A Member of the 29th Engineers wrote this poem describing some of the pleasures one encountered riding in a French box car:

"HOMMES, 40--CHEVEAUX, 8

Roll, roll, roll, over the rails of France
See the world and its map unfurled, five centimes in your pants
What a noble trip, jolt, jog, and jar
Forty we, with equipment C, in one flat wheel box car,
    We are packed by hand,
    Shoved aboard in teens,
    Pour a little oil on us
    And we would be sardines

Rations! Oo-la-la! and how we love the man
Who learned how to intern our chow in a cold and clammy can
Beans and beef and beef, beef and beans and beef,
Willie raw, he will win the war, take in your belt a reef
    Mess kits flown the coop,
    Cups gone up the spout
    Use your thumbs for issue forks
    And pass the bull about.

Hit the floor for bunks, six hommes to one homme's place,
It's no fair to the bottom layer, to kick 'em in the face.
Move the corp'ral's feet out of my left ear,

Lay off, Sarge, you are too large--
I'm not a bedsack, dear,
>   Lift my head up, please,
>   From this bag of bread;
>   Put it on somebody's chest,
>   Then I'll sleep like the dead.

Roll, roll, roll, roll, hammer and snore and fight
Traveling Zoo the whole day through, and bedlam all the night
Four days in the cage, going from hither to hence.
Ain't it great to ride by freight at good old Unc's expense?" --Ex
(24)

Rennes, located just outside of Brest, housed a large lo-
comotive terminal and repair center.

July 26
Moved on all day destination changed to Langres
Station. Sidetracked for some time because of supplies to
Cheatau Theirry [Chateau-Thierry] *Drive. Passed Tours in P.M.*
Not much to see but fields Passed Gun Factory at 7 P.M. "Krup
Factory of France". Left main line and moved all night Had
French coffee served at midnight and tried to sleep d _ _ _
d _ _ _ d _ _ _Passed throu Bourges

Tours was a major railroad and supply hub. The A.E.F.'s
Services of Supply (S.O.S.) was headquartered there.

The allusion to the "Krupps Factory" would lead me to
believe that this French arms factory was a particulary large one.
At the outset of World War I, Germany possessed the most formidable armament industry in Europe. Much of Germany's war-
making capability came from one company, the Krupp Works.
This munitions giant was located in Essen, Germany. The plant
encompassed 60 factory buildings and employed 41,000 workers. The Krupp complex was described as a city inside a city. It
possessed its own street system, police force, fire department,
and traffic laws.(25)

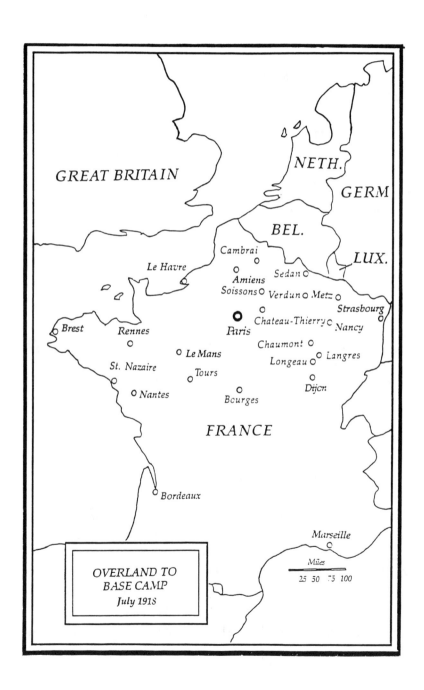

OVERLAND TO
BASE CAMP
July 1918

Two double-track railways from St. Nazaire in the north-west and Bordaux in the southwest met in central France at Bourges. From Bourges, the rail line linked Nevers, Dijon, Neufchateau, and points further into the Lorraine sector.

July 27
Traveled right along during morning.
Reached Dijon at 11:30 Red Cross served coffee and cakes.
Was best ever. Put insupply of eats left 1:30 P.M. in good
spirits. Reached U.S. Camp Wiliams at 4:00 Side tracked
and Red Cross again showed their colors. Was switched
around left 7 P.M. On up grade trip started throu tunnels and
throu cuts till 10:30 P.M. reached Langres at 11:30 P.M.
Trucks carried us to Longue [Longeau].

Trip Route:-
Breste [Brest]*-Rennes-Tours*
Bourges-Dijon-Langres to Longue [Longeau]

Numerous organizations provided support services for American servicemen overseas during World War I. The American Red Cross, the Knights of Columbus, the Salvation Army, the Jewish Welfare Board, and the Young Men's Christian Association (Y.M.C.A.) all played a role in bolstering the war effort in France. To help clarify the functions of each organization, the A.E.F. issued an edict on August 28, 1917. Under what was described as "a guiding rule," the work of relief was assigned exclusively to the Red Cross while the activities of amusement and recreation were delegated to the other groups.

The American Red Cross raised over $400,000,000 between June, 1917 and February, 1919 to meet its needs overseas. Initially, the Red Cross established canteens and huts at ports receiving American troops and at important railroad junctions on the way to the front. Later, it maintained dispensaries and provided bed and bathing facilities for troops in transit or on leave. When needed, the Red Cross also assisted the Medical Corps in the field by contributing supplies and nursing staff.(26)

Second Rest Camp
July 28th _Sunday_

      Reached Barracks with baggage at 3:30 A.M. Turned in at night on floor. Better than box cars. Had little sleep eat breakfast and visited the French village. All of stone-manure piles in the street You judge the hospitality and money of a place by the size of the manure pile. Took shoes off first time in four days and washed hands and face. Not able to take bath or wash any thing. Feeling good but tired. Barracks used before by 165th Infantry of Rain Bow Division on arrival.

      Gen Pershing Passed in auto at retreat.

General John J. Pershing, Commander, A.E.F.

One of the most bizarre customs encountered by American Doughboys was the storage of large manure piles in the front yards of many French homes. In effect, the manure pile was the family bank account. The larger the pile, the more wealthy the landowner. An often-told story relates a common reaction of American troops. In this case, a company of the 28th (Keystone) Division marched into a particularly fragrant French village. The stench was so severe, one soldier commented that the whole town must have been made up of millionaires. The custom was most common in the Vosges region of southern France.(27)

The "Rainbow Division" was created in August, 1917. The War Department ordered the formation of a composite National Guard Division, the 42nd, that would contain a contingent of guard troops from 26 separate states. The states that contributed soldiers to the division included Alabama, California, Colorado, Georgia, Illinois, Indiana, Iowa, Kansas, Louisiana, Maryland, Michigan, Minnesota, Missouri, Nebraska, New Jersey, New York, North Carolina, Ohio, Oklahoma, Oregon, Pennsylvania, South Carolina, Tennessee, Texas, Virginia, Wisconsin, and the District of Columbia. Because of its national composition, the 42nd Division became known as "The Rainbow Division." Initially, the War Department had hoped that the 42nd would be the first American combat unit to enter the fray. This, however, did not come to pass. The 26th Division earned the distinction of being the first A.E.F. division to be sent over to France in 1917.

The 165th Infantry belonged to the 42nd's 83rd Infantry Brigade. The 165th was in actuality the old 69th New York Irish of Civil War fame. The soldiers in this unit were nearly all of Irish descent. Most called Brooklyn their home.(28)

General John J. Pershing was Commander in Chief of the A.E.F. He was born in Laclede, Missouri in 1860 and graduated from West Point in 1886 with a commission in the Cavalry. Pershing saw combat in the Sioux Indian War, the Spanish-American War, and the Philippine Insurrection. As a commander, he led the Moro Expedition in the Philippines and the Punitive Expedition in search of the Mexican outlaw Pancho Villa. Pershing also had stints as a professor of military science at the University of Nebraska, an observer of the Russo-Japanese War, and a military governor of the Moro Province in the southern Philippines. He was promoted to full General on October 6, 1917. Following the World War, Congress named him General of the Armies, and in 1921, he became Chief of Staff of the Army. Pershing officially retired in 1924 and died at the age of 87 in 1948.

General Pershing carried the nickname "Black Jack" for much of his military life. The origin of the nickname can be traced back to West Point where Pershing returned in 1897 as an instructor. Prior to this assignment, as a lieutenant with the 10th Cavalry, he participated in the Sioux Indian War. The troops Pershing commanded were black cavalrymen, the famous "Buffalo Soldiers." When cadets at West Point learned of his former association with black troops, racist elements at the academy labeled Pershing "Nigger Jack." With time, the nickname was toned down to "Black Jack."

Pershing is described by his biographer Frank E. Vandiver as a man who lived life to the fullest. He knew the thrill of ambition as well as the disappointment of missed opportunity. Pershing relished the glory of his achievements yet always retained the basic virtues of a true gentleman. Pershing was a man of wit, humor, and passion--a man who was not afraid to display honest patriotism. From an American historical perspective, to know General John J. Pershing is to know World War I. The two are so intertwined that it is next to impossible to analyze one without the other. Perhaps Pershing had this in mind all along.

World War I historian Samuel L.A. Marshall amplified this fact in his book _World War I_. Pershing dominated the times like no other commander in American history. Although his mental capabilities as a general were no greater than his rivals, Pershing's air of self-confidence and superiority made him the ideal military leader. In public, Pershing's personality was stoic and reserved. He did, however, possess those key character traits that are so crucial when molding men into a cohesive, fighting force. Patience, emotional stability, and fortitude made General Pershing the successful commander he was.(29)

July 29
Was fair day. Good food but not enough. Inspection of rifles at 3:00 P.M. h _ _ _. Put up Military Law. Mayor---named Governor. Lieut Meade as Mayor. Military police by Companies. Light till 9 :30 P.M.
Camp located on huge plataue 1200' A.S.L. [Above Sea Level] *and on main truck line to front from Dijon. Prices high.*

July 30
Clear warm day. Was day of rest. Had Company Bath at 2 P.M. in Canal of the Marne. First bath since the Toloa pumped salt water and first good change since left Wash. Barracks.

July 31
Clear warm. Right to buy light wines granted at soldiers hours 10-1:30 5:00-9:00 Served in wine cellars by little beer maids
Saw the French style of Bull servicing Cow on Main St. of Langres.

Le Terrum Barracks--Y.M.C.A.--Daily schedule-Ptomaine poison--Army Training Engineering School, Fort Longeville, St. Menges--Daily schedule--Training in Flash Ranging

AUGUST 1918

Aug 1918

Aug 1st
      Clear and warm. Company Bath in Canal.
Retreat order to prepare to move 7 A.M. on the morrow

Aug 2nd
      Raining light. Revealry at 5:15 A.M. Off at
7A.M.-11 Kilo's to camp at Langres. "West Point of France"
Reached camp at 10:30 A.M. City walls dated 1844. Only
city not taken in F-P War 1870-1871 and the check.
      Le Tureene Barracks used as Annex Officers training
school.

The U.S. Army Staff College, Langres

General Pershing believed very strongly in imparting
military skills in a school environment. This attitude no doubt
was a reflection of his past assignments as a military instructor at
the University of Nebraska and at West Point. While both the
British and the French did operate military schools in France
during the war, the curriculum they taught was weighted heavily

towards defensive tactics and trench warfare. By September of 1917, heavy reliance on machine guns, mortars, and grenades had nearly made basic rifle marksmanship a lost art among Allied troops. General Pershing was horrified. "It was my opinion," wrote Pershing, "that the victory could not be won by the costly process of attrition, but it must be won by driving the enemy out into the open and engaging him in a war of movement." To counteract this perceived lapse in instruction, General Pershing ordered the creation of a system of schools to indoctrinate American troops with "the fundamentals so thoroughly taught at West Point for a century." The General Staff College in Langres was part of this system. Known to many as the "West Point of France," the General Staff College provided student officers with an intensive three month course covering what General Pershing described as "the details of our own staff organization and administration, our system of supply, and the coordination and employment of our forces in combat."(1)

Langres is located approximately 20 miles south-southeast from Chaumont. The town's rich history reaches back to before the Christian era in Europe. Langres was originally a Roman outpost in the province of Gaul. Situated on high ground, the frontier garrison served as a deterrent to the designs of hostile tribes in the area. Julius Caesar's legions are credited with strengthening the city's walls and constructing a series of twelve macadamized roads radiating out from the town's center. In 52 B.C., on the rolling fields not far from Langres, Caesar scored a major military victory over the followers of Vercingetorix, the most famous Gaulish chieftain to ever rise up against the power of Rome. The city found little respite from military conflict in subsequent years. From the time of Caesar to World War I, Langres was invaded 42 separate times by the Germans.(2)

The Turenne Barracks was located just outside of Langres. It served as a rest area for troops destined for the nine

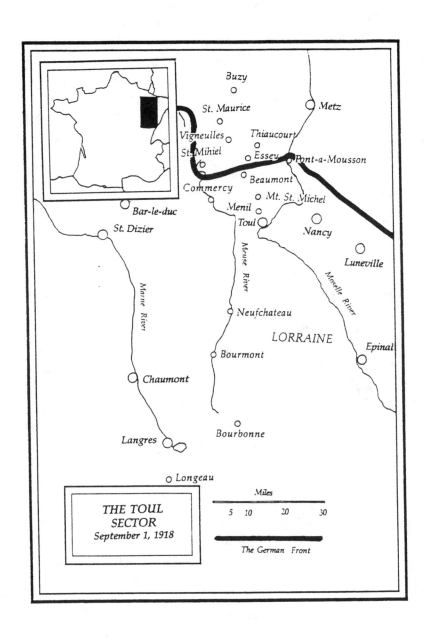

THE TOUL
SECTOR
September 1, 1918

Miles

5   10   20   30

The German Front

kilometer, uphill hike to the Flash and Sound Ranging School at Fort de St. Menge.(3)

Aug 4 Sunday
Clear day marked with showers. Went to Y.M.C.A.   for food. 164th Infantry Band located in Blln 72 and gave concert

The interior of a typical Y. M. C. A. hut

The Young Men's Christian Association (Y.M.C.A.) was one of the first organizations to receive permission from the U.S. Government to set up relief operations among American troops overseas in France. During World War I, 25,926 men and women volunteered for service under the "Red Triangle." The sole purpose of the Y.M.C.A. in wartime was to promote and maintain high morale among American soldiers. To this end, the Y.M.C.A. constructed over 4000 huts, canteens, and Post Exchanges at training installations and posts of embarkation in the U.S., on transport ships crossing the Atlantic, at staging areas throughout Europe, and on the front lines of the battlefield in France. According to the official history of the Y.M.C.A. in World War I, "The aim and the apex of the whole organization was the 'hut.' Everything was centered on the desire to make the Y camps both at home and abroad take the place of the American home, school, club, stage, and church. The 'hut' in hundreds of cases was a a large commodious, especially designed wooden building, uniquely fitted to be the center of the social life of the military community." These Y.M.C.A. institutions offered a myriad of services. Basic ones included the distribution of coffee and dough-nuts, the preparation of holiday meals, the selling of personal items such as cigarettes and toiletries, and the hosting of reli-gious services. On the more elaborate side, the Y.M.C.A. spon-sored athletic contests, vaudeville acts, casinos, and motion pic-tures.(4)

The 164th Infantry was a component of the 82nd Infantry Brigade of the 41st Division. The War Department designated the National Guard troops of Idaho, Montana, Oregon, Washing-ton, North Dakota, South Dakota, Colorado, New Mexico, and Wyoming to form the 41st Division in 1917. The 41st was often referred to as the "Wildcat Division" or the "Western Division." Throughout the war, General Pershing continually sought to im-prove the music provided by American regimental bands. Se-lected members of various regimental bands were often tempo-rarily transferred to Chaumont for intensive instruction with the Headquarters Band. General Pershing believed that stirring mu-sic was a morale-builder especially for troops on the march.(5)

Aug 5
Started drill again
Messer Style

5:45	*First Call*
6:00	*Revealry*
7:30	*Breakfast*
8:00	*Police and Sick Call*
8:30	*Drill and*
12:30	*Fatigue*
1:00	*Dinner*
1:30	*Drill and*
4:30	*Fatigue*
7:00	*Supper*

_8:30_	_Call to Quarters_
_9:00_	_Tatoo_
_9:30_	_Taps_
_10:00_	_All in_

Aug 6th   _Rain-Sun+Drill_

Aug 7th   _Rain-Sun_
       Got first "Over Sea Mail" dated July 9th First issue shoes 5D. Gen Pershing given highest military honor of France.

The presentation of the French Grand Cross of the Legion of Honor to General Pershing, Chaumont, August 6, 1918

General Pershing was presented with the Grand Cross of the Legion of Honor by French President M. Raymond Poincare at Chaumont on August 6. Although the ceremony incorporated all of the usual pomp and circumstance of such military events, it was not without its awkward moments. Pershing recalled that after the medal presentation:

> . . .according to French custom, he kissed me on both cheeks, but not without some difficulty, as he was not so tall as I and it was

necessary for him to rise on tiptoe and for me to lean somewhat forward. . .Without implying the slightest criticism of the form of salutation used in the ceremony, I cannot refrain from confessing my embarrassment, especially as I could hear the restrained laughter of the irreverant Americans in the area who witnessed my situation, no doubt with sympathy. I thought that M. Poincare himself was probably quite as much embarrassed as I was. Moreover, he must have heard the suppressed mirth as plainly as I did.(6)

Aug 8th
>   *Rain-Sun Mail from over sea dated July 15th*

Aug 9th
>   *Rain-Sun Went to hospital got confined to*
quarters for toemain [ptomaine] *poison.*

Ptomaine poisoning is a type of bacterial poisoning caused by the ingestion of spoiled meat.

Aug 10th
>   *Clear warm day Confined to quarters.*

Aug 11th
>   *Clear-warm. Released from quarters. Went*
back to city. Was alive with officers.

Aug 12
>   *Clear-warm. Drill Got Paid 60 Francs 10.50*
Next over Sea 11.30 Company started to bust up. Major
McCumber made Lieut. Colonel.

>   *Entered U.S. Army School at Fort St. Menge*

Aug 13
>   *Left at 8:30 Said good by to Sur Le Turenne Barracks*
(West point of France) 12 kilo hike to Army Training

Eng. School at Ft. Longeville [Ligniville] St. Menge Entered F.+S.

Fort located on top of knol built by Caesar and rebilt 1886 7. Over looks the valley and canal of the Marne. El 340 M.

Officers attached
Capt. Whitney
Lieut Morrow-Mac [McLananan]-*Huston* [Houston]
David
Lieut Simmons [Simons]-*Kester* [Koester]-*Holmes*

The entrance to the Army Engineering School, Langres

The Army's Flash and Sound Ranging School was located at Fort de St. Menge. At the time, the commanding officer at the school was Lieutenant Norman R. French. A member of Company A, 29th Engineers, the first class to train at Fort de St. Menge, recalled the architectural and historical characteristics of the old fortress:

> The historic fort which we now occupied was in existence before the Franco-Prussian War, the north end is in part, the ancient fort. The precipitous hill on which the fortification is constructed, divides the two approaches to Langres from the north,

the greater of which is the Marne Valley. From the crest of the hill it would be possible to rake the surrounding country with gun fire. Every road approaching Langres is 'covered.' The modern fort is named Ligniville, after a Frenchman of noble birth who was commander of the forces in that area. The fort was rebuilt in 1871-1874. As we explored the fort we observed two definite stages of construction, two types of stone work. Many of the terraces for rifle fire are approached by tunnels and bulwarked by masonry, which appears much older than the finer work of the casements

To properly explore the fort would require several days, and many rooms would probably not be visited. There are rooms at all elevations, from the gun rooms and lookouts on the crown of the fort approximately 40 feet deep. The number of gun mounts are large and all reached by an ingenious underground passage of one type or another. The fort presents all secret passages and mystic chambers that the most romantic could desire.(7)

Officers of the 29th Engineers:

Captain Eric F. Whitney, Portland, Oregon

First Lieutenant John D. McLanahan, Princeton, New Jersey

Second Lieutenant Joseph David, Muskegon, Michigan

First Lieutenent Edmond G. Simons, Eutawville, South Carolina

Aug 14

Entered Flash Section of Am. Gen. Intelegant Division at Army Eng. School.

Routine

5:45	*First Call*
6:00	*Revealry*
6:20	*Breakfast*
7:20	*Exercise*
8:30	*School*
11:30	
12:00	*Dinner*
12:45	*School*
5:00	
5:50	*Retreat*

6:00   *Supper*
10:30   *Taps*
School three nights a week 7:30 to 10
Baths usable   9:30-11:00
                 1:-   *4:-*
                 7:-   *8:-*
School in Charge of
Lieut French
"   *Dow*
Master Eng. Pettee

Members of the 29th Engineers engaging in a friendly game of craps,
Langres, August 24, 1918

Members of the 29th Engineers:
Captain Norman R. French, Fort Fairfield, Maine
First Lieutenant Leonard M. Dow, Knoxville,
       Tennessee

Allen D. Pettee, Co. B, Philadelphia, Pennsylvania

Aug 15
    Clear+warm School

Aug 16
    Clear+warm 3 <u>Mo</u> Entered Army School

Aug 17
Clear+warm Inspection 2 P.M.

Aug 18   Sunday
Clear and warm (Chatau Thierry [Chateau Thierry] *drive started July 18th)*

Aug 19th
Clear and warm American Army landed in Russia. School. Am+Fr officers vistied Sch.

Russia was in the throes of civil war. The fragile Provisional Government that emerged after the removal of Tsar Nicholas II had collapsed. The Bolsheviks who had been instrumental in the 1917 Revolution seized power in Moscow, negotiated a separate peace with Germany, and were in the process of consolidating their grip over the rest of Russia. Opposing this takeover in the frontier regions were no less than six White armies composed of various democratic and socialist factions, and a legion of volunteers from Czechoslovakia that had initially been sent to Russia to counter the German invasion at the start of the World War. Fearful of Lenin's vow to extend the Bolshevik Revolution worldwide, 14 foreign countries sent 160,000 soldiers to assist in the battle against the Reds.

On June 1, 1918, without any consultation with Congress and against the advice of his military advisors, President Woodrow Wilson ordered the deployment of American troops to northern Russia. He cited two specific reasons for his decision: the need to guard Allied supplies and Russian railroads from German seizure and the need to save the Czech volunteers who were trying to return to their homeland. While these may have been worthy objectives, they were not in reality the determining factors in Wilson's mind. Concern over Japanese influence in Siberia and a desire to work in consort with other Allied nations in Russia were no doubt high on Wilson's agenda. Perhaps the most important reason for American intervention, however, was Wilson's hope of destroying the Bolshevik regime, a regime whose ideology threatened Wilson's dream of a new postwar world.

The United States committed nearly 20,000 troops to the civil war in Russia. The first American troops to serve participated in the Allied invasion of the northwestern port of Archangel on August 1. Marines from the *U.S.S. Olympia* joined a detachment of British Royal Marines and a French infantry regiment in securing the city. Four days later, elements of the U.S. 339th Infantry Regiment of the 85th Division landed in Archangel. This unit which had been training in Britain for service in France hit Russian soil bearing a Polar Bear shoulder insignia and carrying American-made, Russian "long rifles."

A second contingent of American troops later was dispatched to the western port of Vladivostok on the Pacific Ocean. The unit designated for the mission was the 8th Division under the command of General William Graves. Two advance regiments of infantry previously stationed in Manila, the 27th and the 31st, arrived in Vladivostok in mid-August, around the time of this entry. The rest of the 8th Division, some 5,000 troops, sailed from San Francisco and reached the Russian port on September 1.

The American presence in Russia continued after the Armistice officialy ended World War I. The intervention, however, was to no avail. The Bolshevik armies continued to advance throughout Russia as the White armies disintegrated. After fighting longer and more continuously than any other unit had fought on the Western Front in France, the 339th Infantry Regiment pulled out of Archangel on August 5, 1919. The last contingent of the 8th Division based in Siberia left Vladivistok on April 1, 1920.(8)

Aug 20th
    Mail form over sea Clear+warm School
      Transferred to Co. D 29th Eng F-R-C [Company D, 29th Engineers, Flash Ranging Company]

Aug 21
Clear+Warm Great movement of troops on R.R

Aug 22
Clear+warm Temp 90-School

Aug 23
Clear+warm Spent half day Artilary started in
Toul Sector

Aug 24
Clear+warm Exam in Flash Got gas Drill

Both the Central Powers and the Allies used toxic gas warfare during World War I. The first tactical use of gas in battle occurred on January 31, 1915. The German Ninth Army fired specially designed artillery shells filled with chlorine in a barrage attack on Russian troops at Bolimow. The attack was a failure. German technicians had yet to realize that poison gas was harmless in sub-zero weather. Nearly three months later, German forces did use poison gas successfully on the Western Front at Ypres, France. "The Great Gas Attack" commenced on April 22. Emitted by cylinders lobbed near the Allied lines, the greenish yellow, chlorine gas spread quickly in only 15 minutes. Those caught in the thickest part of the cloud died a slow, painful death. Pandemonium immediately broke out among the 15,000 French and Canadian troops stationed in the front trenches. The Germans, however, underestimated their new weapon and did not press the Ypres salient as forcefully as they should have. Had the Germans followed up the gas barrage with a substantial advance, Ypres could have been a very serious defeat for the Allies.

Various agents were utilized in gas warfare. Chorine and phosgene were two chemicals that produced a high number of casualties. Both gasses attacked the lungs. Although chlorine was used early in the war, phosgene became more widely used because its killing dose was half that of chlorine. Shells containing chlorine or phosgene were often marked with white crosses. Mustard gas or dichlorethyl sulphide was another agent often used during the war. This corrosive chemical which had the slight odor of mustard burned through gas masks, clothing, and human flesh. Whereas chlorine and phosgene usually dissipated in a relatively short time, mustard gas clung on anything it fell onto and often claimed its victims hours after exposure. Assorted forms of tear gas were also used during the war. They were much cheaper in cost than the killer agents. While these bromine gasses merely irritated eye membranes, they nonetheless caused enemy units to don protective gear which greatly reduced their fighting capability.(9)

> **_Aug 25 Sunday_**
> **_Clear and cool S. R. S. #4 left for mobile work._**

Sound Ranging Section #4 combined men who had gained experience in one of the three previously organized sound ranging sections and men from Company D of the 29th Engineers who had just completed training at Fort de St. Menge. The unit entered the lines at Foret de Amblonville near Verdun on October 20, 1918.(10)

> **_Aug 26_**
> **_Clear + warm   School_**

> **_Aug 27_**
> **_Clear + warm   School_**

> **_Aug 28_**
> **_Clear + cool (Detachment transferred to Co. D 29th Eng.) Aug 20_**

> **_Aug 29_**
> **_Clear + cool Read over Sea Mail of July 27th_**

32 days   School

    Aug 30
        Clear + cool Sound back from mobile
operations

    Aug 31
        Clear + cool Exam on Flash Work Signed
payroll 11.30 64.40 Fr.

    Finish Course Rated as observer +
Computor for F.R. S.

*Mobile operations in Marne Valley--Toul Sector Drive--
Overseas Theater--29th Engineers reformed--"Out of the
West"--Summary of dates--Clemenceau--Sections and Marks
of the A.E.F.--Notes on outfits--Division marks--Aeroplane
marks--"Soldiers of Germany"--"A Prayer"--"Only a
Volunteer"--Toul--St. Mihiel--Mt. Sec--Codes*

SEPTEMBER 1918

Sept.

Sept 1 Sunday
*   Clear + cool. Short Arms inspection. Read over sea mail Aug 10th-(21 days)*

Sept 2 Monday Labor Day
*   I remember Sept 1912*
F.R.S. #3 left for mobile operations along Marne Valley

Private Pfennig initially belonged to Flash Ranging Section No. 3. It was composed of men from Company D, 29th Engineers.(1)

Sept 3 Clear + cool
*   Central-Mardoi*
Loire   "   Marac
Sept. 4
*   5*
*   6*
*   7   Manuvers ended.*
Sgt. Baldwin. Sgt Bogart 75 mm-9 shots on trajectory at one time. 15 shots per minute for 15 minute record.

The French 75mm light artillery piece

Members of the 29th Engineers:
John C. Baldwin, Co. B, Garden City, Long Island
John Bogart, Co. C, Brooklyn, New York

When appointed commander of the A.E.F., General Pershing sought to field a complete army under the control of American officers. An issue that immediately concerned him was the procurement of artillery for use in France. At the start of the war, American artillery was technologically backward. Most of the weapons in existence were of the three inch variety. About 540 of these outdated field guns were scattered in outposts across the U.S. and the Philippine Islands and largely unavailable for immediate use. Heavier guns were nonexistent. The Ordnance Department had been long negligent in developing new artillery models. While Pershing hoped that American manufacturers would eventually fill the void in the long run, he realized that his army would have to rely on foreign-made pieces for at least two years. Pershing concluded that the adoption of the French pieces rather than British versions made the most sense given the fact that most American divisions would be operating in close relation with French units.

The workhorse of most American artillery units was the French-made 75mm Puteaux field gun. This light artillery piece, officially designated the M1, was first developed in 1897. The 75mm gun had a range of 9,350 yards using common steel shells and 7,440 yards using 16 pound shrapnel ammunition. It possessed two revolutionary design features that made possible a very high rate of fire. The first was a screw breech block. With the simple turning of a handle, a skilled crew could uncover the bore, insert a cartridge into the breech, and recover the breech block with great rapidity. The second feature was a long-recoil cylinder. This mechanism consisted of a piston that moved between two cylinders, one filled with oil and the other with pressurized air. The device absorbed the energy of the recoil and returned the gun to battery position without disturbing the position of the gun carriage. Ironically, the long-recoil cylinder was the invention of a Krupp engineer, Konrad Haussner. It was never adapted to German guns because the Krupp Works and the German government labeled it "impractible for use in the field." Under optimum conditions, the 75mm field gun was capable of being fired at a rate of 20 shots a minute, a shot every three seconds. One American artilleryman claimed his comrades "became so proficient in loading that the Germans afterward frequently declared they were using a 3-inch machine gun."(2)

> *Sept 8th Sunday*
> > *Rain Snow and cool Got Paid 63.50 11.30*
> *5.65 on 1*
> > *Chaplain Dewart. U.S. 77 Art. give lecture at*
> *YM. "Women and the War"*

Chaplain Dewart belonged to the 77th Field Artillery Brigade of the 4th Division. One can surmise that the real topic of his lecture was sexual continence. General Pershing was quite concerned about the spread of venereal disease among American troops. In his memoirs, Pershing outlined orders designed to limit the effect of venereal disease on the A.E.F.:

> One of the important duties of the Medical Department was the prevention and cure of venereal disease, which in all other wars had caused serious reductions in effectives. Its prevalence in the Allied armies presented no exception to previous experience. From the purely practical standpoint of difficulty in replacing men, the possiblility of having large numbers of ineffectives from this cause could not be contemplated without making every effort to prevent it. Among the first meaures taken to restrict the evil was the promulgation of very stringent regulations in which medical officers and all others were enjoined to impress continence upon our troops, not only as a military obligation but as a patriotic duty.
> Commanding officers were directed to encourage and promote high moral standards of living among the members of their commands. General orders placed the responsibility for good conduct directly upon the soldier himself and prescribed that where men became unfit for duty through misconduct summary punishment would

follow. The question was destined to give us considerable concern because of the difference between the French attitude and our own regarding the supression of sources of infection, but our efforts on the whole were remarkable successful. The percentage of ineffectives in our army from this cause was much lower than that of the Allies and surpassed any previous record in the history of wars. (3)

**Sept 9**

    **Clear + warm**

**Transport Mt. Vernon Torpedoed but still afloat. One of boats in our convoy. Was (Kronprinzessin Cecile) of North German Lloyds 635.4 beam 72.3 HP 33 000 depth 40.8**

On the morning of September 5, 1918, the transport ships _Mount Vernon_ and _Agememnon_ were located some 250 miles from the French port of Brest. The ships were steaming back to America under heavy destroyer escort when they came under submarine attack. A single torpedo tore a 19 foot diameter hole in the _Mount Vernon_ amidships. Although 7,000 tons of seawater poured through the giant gash, the ship miraculously stayed afloat. The _Mount Vernon_ was successfully towed back to Brest on September 6. In the attack, 37 sailors perished. Later in October, after repairs were made, the _Mount Vernon_ resumed its journey across the Atlantic.(4)

**Sept 10th**

    **Rain + cool   Co D 79th Eng   S R S #4 left for front**

**Sept 11**

    **Rain +   cool   Read mail oversea   2 Mo-over Sea was winning Eng**

    **weight   58 kilo**

                      **128 lbs**

   **Toul Sector**

**July 12th**

    **Clear + cool**

Toul Sector Drive started At 1:55 Gen Pershing fired first gun. 2:00 Hell let loose.

"Wilson's Billion dollar barrage"

Took Mt Sec by going around. Cost French 35 000 men to hold 15 min in 1914.

Battery C, 6th Field Artillery fired the first shot of the Saint Mihiel barrage. Mount Sec, a strategic highland, is in the distance.

The scope of "Wilson's Billion dollar barrage" can best be illustrated by the following chart:

EXPENDITURE OF ARTILLERY AMMUNITION IN
MODERN BATTLES

Year	Battle	Day's Duration	Army	Rounds Expended
1863	Chickamagua	2	Union	7,325
1863	Gettysburg	3	Union	32,781
1870	St. Privat	1	German	39,000
1904	Nan Sam	1	Japanese	34,047
1904	Sha Ho	9	Russian	274,360
1915	Neuve Chapelle	3a	British	197,000
1915	Souches	1b	French	300,000
1916	Somme	7c	British	4,000,000
1917	Messines Ridge	7c	British	2,753,000
1918	St. Mihiel	4b	American	1,093,217

a. Artillery preparation lasted 35 minutes
b. Artillery preparation lasted 4 hours.
c. Artillery preparation intermittent 7 days. (5)

The Toul Sector drive is more commonly referred to as the reduction of the Saint Mihiel salient. In June of 1917, General Petain and General Pershing agreed that the first free-standing American armies to enter the war in France should take up positions in the Lorraine. From this sector, U.S. forces could freely strike out toward fronts near Verdun or Nancy. There was, however, one obstacle that would have to be overcome before the Allies could threaten either front. It was the Saint Mihiel salient. This German-controlled bulge of land flanked both fronts in the Lorraine. Within it lay railway lines that the Allies would ultimately have to control in order to supply their armies operating near Verdun or Nancy. Both Petain and Pershing concurred that the reduction of the salient should be an American operation, and Pershing instructed his Chief of Operations, Colonel George C. Marshall, to draw up a battle plan that could be implemented in the following spring or summer.

As the summer of 1918 progressed, preparation for the reduction of the Saint Mihiel salient intensified. On August 15, Colonel Marshall delivered what he thought would be the final draft of the plan to General Pershing, now self-appointed commander of the U.S. First Army. The plan was then passed on to Supreme Allied Commander Marshall Foch for final approval. He supported it and officially assigned 25 divisions, 19 American and six French, to the task. All would fight under Pershing's command. The attack would commence on September 12.

Events late in August, however, drastically changed the scope of the Saint Mihiel assault for Pershing and the Americans. Fighting had intensified near Cambrai on the Aisne River. Marshall Foch hoped to pour more Allied manpower into the region as soon as possible to exploit perceived enemy weaknesses. With this in mind, Foch approached Pershing on August 30 and proposed splitting the American army in two following the

Saint Mihiel operation. Half would be sent into the Argonne to fight alongside the French, and the other half would fight under French command in the Champagne sector. Pershing vehemently opposed the idea. The general would not tolerate the division of an American army he had labored so hard to assemble. Two days later, Foch and General Petain returned to Pershing with a compromise. The French generals accepted Pershing's desire to keep American forces intact. Indeed, they argued, U.S. armies should be allowed to fight independently as long as they operated within the grand scheme laid down by Foch. At this point, Foch's "grand scheme" called for a British attack toward Cambrai and a two-pronged French drive across the Aisne. American forces would reduce the Saint Mihiel salient, cease the attack no matter the response of the Germans, and redeploy in the Argonne. Pershing agreed to the new strategy and ordered Colonel Marshall to make necessary alterations in the original plan as to facilitate the newly-conceived Argonne operation.

This would be no small task. In a mere 14 days, the bulk of the U.S. First Army would have to be moved from the Metz front to that of the Meuse-Argonne. Later, Marshall would recollect in his memoirs that he could not remember a historical situation where the fighting of one battle by one army had been preceded by the planning for a future battle to be fought by that same army on a different front. In this case, troops already chosen to participate in the first operation had been issued orders to ultimately transfer to another field of combat. It was now clear that the attack on the Saint Mihiel would be a mere prelude to the U.S. drive into the Argonne.

Upon first appearance, the Saint Mihiel salient looked very formidable. The land to be liberated was located between the Meuse and Moselle Rivers. It was roughly the shape of a triangle with points at Pont-a-Mousson, St. Mihiel, and Verdun. The geographical lay of the land seemed to favor the German occupiers. On the west, the German line was anchored on the Cotes-de-Meuse. The heights of Montsec and Loupmont on the southern flank gave the Germans superior observation over the plain to the west. The central part of the salient consisted of crater-filled terrain near the town of Thiaucourt and potentially swampy wetlands on the Woevre Plain. The entire area was laced with streams whose depths were unknown. Anchoring the salient in the rear was the fortress of Metz. German fortifications were solid throughout the region. Five defensive positions, including the infamous Hiddenburg Line, would meet an invading enemy on the way to Metz. Each contained heavily revetted trenches and artillery-proof troop shelters. The entire network appeared to be covered with impenetrable barbed wire.

For most of 1918, fighting along the salient had been sporadic at worst. Trench lines nearly half a mile apart made for remarkably quiet evenings. American troops on the front often travelled into the no-man's-land at night to listen to Geman brass bands play in the distance. Patrols mounted by both sides seemed more interested in looking for intelligence than engaging in firefights. Nonetheless, tranquility could be and often was shattered by unannounced artillery barrages. Deadly artillery duals could last for hours at a time. The frequent use of gas made thse exchanges all the more uncomfortable for soldiers in gas gear who literally had to sweat it out in the trenches. The sitting and waiting existence most American soldiers experienced in the summer of 1918 along the Saint Mihiel salient, however, would soon be radically altered in September. An inflow of troops and material and the increase in drill and activity signalled something was afoot. That something remained a mystery to most U.S. servicemen until the early morning of September 12.

What was a mystery to most U.S. troops at the time was a foregone conclusion to their German counterparts. In spite of great effort on the part of the Americans to conceal the buildup of forces opposite Saint Mihiel--the nearly half a million men moved at night and were sheltered during the day in forests to avoid detection by air--spies operating behind the lines made German commander General von Fuchs well aware of American intentions. Initially, Fuchs greeted news of the attack. He had nine experienced, battle-hardened divisions in the line which included a division and two brigades from the Metz group, four divisions of the Bavarian I Corps, three divisions of the Combres group, and the V Corps. With this force, Fuchs hoped to smash the inexperienced Americans in a sweeping counterattack once they had been drawn onto the Woevre Plain. On September 9, however, Fuch's bravado gave way to real concern. He finally came to realize what Pershing had thought all along concerning the strength of the salient--the bulge could be cracked by a coordinated attack along both its flanks. German intelligence reports indicated that the large American force massing to the south was positioning itself to do just that. Only 24 hours later, German heavy guns and equipment began to stream northward. German troops soon followed. The entire salient was evacuated by September 18.

General Pershing learned of the withdrawl only hours before the scheduled attack. News of the planned evacuation to the Hiddenburg Line was contained in documents captured by an American patrol. Fearful that the element of surprise had been lost and that the enemy could then possibly reinforce the salient with an additional four reserve divisions, Pershing decided to commence the assault with an unusually brief artillery barrage of only four hours. The I Corps consisting of the 82nd, 90th, 5th, and 2nd Divisions would begin the attack on the eastern flank of the salient. Simultaneously, the V Corps composed of the 26th and 4th Divisions and the 15th French Colonial Division would press in from the west. At the tip of the salient, the French II Colonial Corps made up of the 39th and 26th Infantry Divisions and the 2nd Cavalry Dismounted Division would hold down German troops at the center. In reserve, Pershing had at his disposal three additional divisions, the 35th, the 91st, and the 80th. All told, Allied forces amounted to 665,000 troops, 3,220 artillery pieces, 1,500 planes, and 267 light tanks. In spite of this massive array of firepower, American analysts expected at least 50,000 Allied casualties.

September 12 arrived in foggy, drizzly darkness. The Allied bombardment broke the stillness at 1 a.m. Although heavy, it lasted only the prescribed four hours. At 5 a.m., troops from I Corps leapt out of their trenches under the cover of a rolling barrage. They swept through broken ground quickly, overran numerous enemy trenches, and collected thousands of German prisoners. In seven hours, I Corps secured its first day territorial objectives and had liberated the towns of Fey-en-Haye, Vieville-en-Haye, and Thiacourt. V Corps had an equally easy time of it. Its goal was achieved at 7 a.m. IV Corps experienced tougher German resistance but still reached its objective line by noon. By the afternoon, intelligence reports indicated that the Americans had caught the Germans offguard while they were in the midst of their retreat. The once orderly movement of German troops and material northward was now breaking down into a crowded, disorganized scramble towards Metz. To cut off as much of the fleeing German army as possible, Pershing ordered the IV and V Corps to push on through the night. By 8:15 p.m., elements of the 26th and the 1st Divisions linked in the town of Vignuelles. Six hours later, the Saint Mihiel salient was in U.S. control. For the next three days, American units participated in mopping up exercises within the newly-freed territory. The new front created by the reduction of the salient now extended roughly on a line which linked Haudimont, Fresens-en-Woevre, Doncourt, Jualny, and Vandieres.

The first German prisoners captured in the Saint Mihiel advance,
Beaumont, September 12, 1918

The speed at which the American infantry units moved over heavily barbed wire defenses was perhaps the biggest surprise of the battle. Using conventional bangolore torpedoes (long tin or sheet-iron tubes containing T.N.T.) and chicken wire, U.S. troops broke through fortifications that their Allied counterparts would have bombarded for days before even contemplating an infantry advance. One astonished French officer commented to Colonel Marshall after the amazing exploit that he was convinced by the evidence on the ground that U.S. infantry had literally walked over the wire. He attributed this remarkable fact to the large feet of the typical American soldier.

The Saint Mihiel operation was a complete success by all accounts. At the expense of only 7,000 Allied casualties, 16,000 prisoners were taken, 450 artillery pieces captured and 200 square miles of territory was liberated. In Pershing's judgement, the spoils of this victory could have been even larger. He wrote in his diary after the battle, "Without a doubt, an immediate continuation of the advance would have carried us well beyond the Hindenburg Line and possibly into Metz, and the temptation to press on was very great, but we would have probably become involved and delayed the greater Meusse-Argonne operation." Indeed, the real significance of the Saint Mihiel saliant reduction would ultimately be tied to the Argonne operation. The American position on the Woevre Plain which appeared to threaten the fortress of Metz allowed the last large campaign of the war to begin in the Argonne.(6)

Sept 13th
> *Clear + cool Moved from Fort to Langres.*
> *Drive ended. 40 000 prisoners.*
> *July 1st 175 000 prisoners to date*

Sept 14th
> *Clear + cool*
> *Worked*

French and American officers along the Hindenburg Line viewing the fortress city of Metz, September 13, 1918

Sept 15   **Sunday**
         Clear + warm   **Toul Sect drive reached its**
objective.

Elements of the 1st Division advancing through the Saint Mihiel salient, September 15, 1918

Sept 16
        Clear + cool
Was on guard from 5 P.M. -8 A. M. Was most beautiful night
Aero-alarm sounded 10:30 Resounded 11:45 No objective
reached. Americans have cleaned Turenne Bks. Some W.C.
Wash Stand-Showers-Wash Room. Went about Army Classes
        4 Months in Army.

Sept 17
        Clear + cool Went into city. Same time
registration day for 1920 class
        Next day to camp--All Amer-French Flags.

Sept 18
        Rain - warm Good thundershowers.
Was laoding paper. 600 lb. detail-700 000 000 sheets
for Eng's in France. Aeor very plentiful over head. Pretty
sight.

Sept 19
        Rain and warm.

Sept 20
        Rain and cool
        Oversea Theater Leauge presented "Laugh Barrage"
        Paula Sherman watch your step

Condon-Chin-Chin-Chow
Pvt. R.R. Conley died at hospital 13 of phnemonia

The first unit of American "Over There" Theater League entertainers

In an effort to boost the morale of U.S. troops stationed overseas during World War I, the Y.M.C.A. created the Entertainment Service. In two years time, this organization evolved into the largest theatrical enterprise ever assembled in history:

It mobilized a personnel of 1470 entertainers (augumented by an estimate of 15,000 soldier-entertainers) for overseas service alone; while in the home camps many times this number volunteered their services to the Y stage. These entertainers included a large proportion of the best known dramatic and musical artists in the United States. It has been estimated that 20,000 professionals and non-professionals made appearances in the home camps.

It gave upward of 220,000 separate performances to the soldiers with an approximate attendance overseas of 88,000,000 and more than 48,000,000 at home.

It provided overseas alone 23,000 costumes and accessories, 18,000 musical instruments, and 450,000 pieces of sheet music.

It sent out stock companies and soldier shows throughout the area of theAmerican Army. It organized four great 'play factories' which were centers for rehearsals, and costume equipment.

It improvised plays and vaudeville acts.

It trained or assisted more than 4000 soldiers to entertain their own troops with soldier shows, it being estimated that 15,000 soldiers appeared in entertainment service.

It sent 135 'song leaders' to France, 1000 athletic directors were also trained as song leaders and augmented the service at home and overseas.

It sent 200 lecturers to France--among them some of the most eminent public speakers in America.

It ran in the Leave Areas and important cities behind the fighting line the largest circuit of casinos and amusement halls ever administered under one management.

It gave overseas 157,000 movie shows aggregating over 8,000,000 feet, or more than 1500 miles of film. The aggregate attendance at these movie shows alone (between April, 1918, and July, 1919) was over 94,000,000 at 5261 different places.

It is estimated that in the United States and overseas the gross attendance at motion pictures reached 210,000,000.

The theater arm of the Entertainment Service was called the Over There Theater League. This brainchild of E.H. Sothern and Winthrop Ames was officially formed on April 13, 1918 at the Palace Theater in New York City. They chose noted American dramatist James Forbes to oversee the entire enterprise. It was his job to recruit the performers who would put on the various shows. Actors, opera singers, magicians, jugglers, comedians, dancers, musicians, playwrights, stage directors, dramatic coaches, advance men, and theater managers began to arrive in France in August of 1918. Once overseas, troupes of entertainers rotated through the various regions of France, in many cases performing not far from the fighting front. At one point in May of 1919, there were over 700 separate productions being performed by groups ranging from dozen man troupes to stock companies like the "Argonne Players."(7)

An epidemic of Spanish influenza broke out among German troops in the summer of 1918. This particular strain of influenza was particularly virulent and proved to be unresponsive to normal treatments. The virus spread quickly through the unsanitary trench system along the front, into rear units of the German army, and finally into the German civilian population itself.

Those unlucky enough to contract this type of influenza suffered through high fever, severe chills, and extreme chest congestion. Death all too often followed as a result of pneumonia. By the late summer, the influenza had degraded the fighting efficiency of most German units considerably. Allied commanders knew this fact and no doubt timed their major offensives in the fall of 1918 with that in mind.

In time, the influenza was passed onto Allied armies as well, first to the French and British and then finally to the American. The epidemic swept through much of the A.E.F. in the latter half of September 1918. It reached its peak the week of October 5th when over 16,000 new cases were reported. During the entire outbreak, nearly 70,000 soldiers were hospitalized, many developing a serious form of pneumonia. The A.E.F. as a whole experienced an influenza mortality rate of 32 percent of cases. For some groups, the rate was as high as 80 percent.

Eventually, Spanish influenza not only plagued the continent of Europe but the entire world. The illness reached the shores of the U.S. in the fall of 1918. Returning troops carried it with them to port cities like New York, Boston, and Baltimore. There, the influenza ravage entire urban populations. Especially hard-hit were immigrant peoples who lived in cramped and unsanitary tenement buildings. In New York, the ferocity of the influenza outbreak prompted journalists to label it "The Great Plague of 1918." Eventually, the flu spread across the entire country. Over 500,000 Americans died. In total, this outbreak of Spanish influenza claimed 20 million victims worldwide before it mysteriously vanished in 1919.(8)

> **Sept 21**
>   **_Rain and cool_**
> **_Work-Work-Work_**

> **Sept 22**   **_Sunday_**
>   **_Rain-clear-cool_**

Co D 29th Engineers reformed composed of F + S-Ranging Sect.

Co B, C, D, E, 29th Eng's F + S-R Sect-2nd Battalion Full Moon.

The 2nd Battalion of Flash and Sound Rangers was officially authorized on August 17. The commanding officer was Theodore Lyman. Headquarters for the unit was located in Toul.(9)

Sept 23 Cool + Rain K. P. duty for day. Rest of Co, came from fort ready to move. Some of Co left for Chaumont headquarters of Commander Chief's of A.E.F.-G.H.Q.

A.E.F. Headquarters, Chaumont

K.P. is an abbreviation for "kitchen police." The military term was coined in the U.S. around 1915. The meaning of the word "police" has nothing to do with law enforcement. In this usage, it refers to cleaning up a designated area--in this case the kitchen and dining areas.

In August of 1917, General Pershing selected Chaumont to be the site of his General Headquarters. The town is located near the upper Marne River on a plateau which overlooks the entire region. Pershing chose it primarily because of its superior location. In addition to being on the line of American communications to the front, Chaumont was also centrally located near probable sectors of American operations. The town of 15,000 also possessed a fine regimental barracks which could furnish ample office space for the headquarters and generous billeting accomodations for American officers in private homes. Historically, Chaumont was the scene of a conference in 1814 where monarchs of Great Britain, Austria, Russia, and Prussia decided the fate of Napoleon.(10)

Sept 24

     Cloudy + cool Nothing doing except latrine dope floating.

Sept 25

     Sunny-cool Was office oderly Read over sea mail Ruth 8-23 Home 8-27 Saw fountains in French Park- 108 AB

Sept 26

     Clear + cool Ammunition train went north
Heaven-Hell or Hoboken by Christmas
Reported actives on Metz Sector. 800 A.F.S. [American Flash Service] *were read commisions*

     End of Service in S.O.S
States to Front
     May 16th 1918 Sept 26th, 1918*
     4 Months-10 Days
*France to Front ***
     July 8th   *Sept. 26th*
     2 Months-18 Days

The Services of Supply (S.O.S.) was a branch of the A.E.F. that carried out the functions of procurement, supply, transportation, and construction.

Out of the West

"Mother what means
the khaki boat
Which comes across the sea?"
"The khaki boat means life+hope
And peace+liberty
Come fast, come fast,
O Khaki lads
Across the brave blue sea"

"Mother, what means
the laden ships
which sail so speedily"?

The laden ships mean wheat and bread
For starving you+me
Sail on , Sail on, O steady ships
The children cry for thee

"Mother what means
the scarlet cross
Upon its field of white?"

"The scarlet cross is mercy's sign
Against a world of night,
Point up, point up,
O scarlet cross
To the Eternal Light."

Mary Putnam Hart.

Summary of Dates

*May	16	Inlisted Co D 29th Eng.
June	5	Co F 603d 79 Div.
July	8	Left Wash Bks.
	10	Sailed on T from H.
	21	Landed at B--
	25	Left B at 6 A.M.

Trip-Rennes Tours-Dijon-Langres
Camp at Longue [Longeau]

Aug	2	Left Logue [Longeau] and made

camp at Langres

	7	First over sea mail
	13	Entered Flash School
	28	Changed Co D 29th Eng
Sept	7	Completed Course Ft. St. Menge
	11	Weight-58 Kilogr.
		128 lbs.
	12	Toul Sector drive started
2 A.M.		
	13	Left Fort for Langres
	27	Left Turenne Barracks
	28	Langres to Toul
*	29	Toul to German Village behind

the lines.

Oct.		
	1	Moved out to billet at Post #2
SROT-F. R. S. #3		
	2	Took over Post #+Sect.
	7	Attached to F.R.S. #2 (Howe

Post.)

	6	German Peace Move
	13	2nd Peace pull

		15	*Turned up side down*
	22-25		*Wilson sent stiff*
			reply to Kaiser and people in
			" to theirs of 22<u>nd</u>

Nov. 1<u>st</u> Austria in revolt stated by authority

	1	*Turkey surrendered*
	4	*Austria signed Armistice*
	6	*Allies give Germany terms*
	8	*German Representative came*

over no-mans land for terms.

	10	*Armistice Signed Unofficial*

22:00

		11	*" " " 5:20*
		11	*Hostilities ceased at 11:00*
	x	18	*Started with Army of*
			Occupation
		22	*Dudelange Luxembourg*
	XDec	7	*F.R.S. #2 to Co D 29<u>th</u> Eng*
		11	*Co D 29 to Co D 74<u>th</u> "*
		11	*Made 1st Cl*
		21	*Left Toul*
		23	*Reached St. Nazair* [St. Nazaire]

(Donges)

	27	*Moved Donges to Nantes*
	31	*Base Hospital #216*

"1919" Cont.

Jan.	1	*New Years in B.H. #216*
Feb.	17	*Left Base Hos. 216*
		Reported to Co. 74<u>th</u> Engs.
	22	*Final Inspection*
	24	*Sailed on Nansemond*
		From St. Nazare[St. Nazaire]
March	11	*Landed at Newport News Va.*
		Camp Stuart

[Editor's Note: This entry appears to have been written in at a chronologically later date.]

"France will never forget that it was at the moment where the struggle was at its hardest that the valiant American troops joined in with ours"

Clemenceau

French Premier Georges Clemenceau reading the latest message from the Front

Georges Benjamin Clemenceau was born in the French town of Vendee in 1841. After receiving a medical education, Clemenceau became a journalist. In 1865, he served as a war correspondent in the U.S. He travelled with Ulysses S. Grant's army. Clemenceau returned to France after his assignment in America, was elected mayor of Montmartre, and wrote for the newspaper *L'Aurore*. In the 1870's, Clemenceau became the leader of the radical party in France. He was appointed Minister of the Interior in 1906. In that same year, Clemenceau was named Premier, a post he held until 1909. The "Tiger" returned to the national spotlight in 1917 at the age of 76 when he became both Premier and Minister of War. Clemenceau held both titles until 1920. He died nine years later.

My Diary
at the
Front

F.R.S.   **#3**   ***Sept. 27***
                  #2   ***Oct. 7***

Sect. & Marks of A.E.F.

*	**F.R.S.**	**Flash Rangeing Service**
*	**S.R.S.**	**Sound " "**
	A.I.S.	**American Inteligant Service**
	S.O.S.	**Service of Supplies**
	R.C.	**Red Cross**
	A.O.A.	**Area of Advance**
	A.P.M.	**Amer Provo Marshal**
	S.R.O.T.	**Service Rangeing Out-Post Terrain**
	R.T.O	**Railroad Trans. Officer**
	M.P.	**Military Police**

> **M.P.E.S.**
> **P.C.**   *Post Commander*
>
> **Notes of Sections**
>
> **Outfits etc.**
>   **S.R.O.T**   **#88**   **#63**
>   **T.P.S.**
>   **A.I.S.**
>   **2nd Eng-Chi. Th.**
>   **Marines 2-D-13th**
>   **Wild Cat Div-Western**
>   **Rainbow Div-Eastern 42 Div.**
>   **Red Diamond-1st Army 5th Div.**
>   **301-302-303**
>   **N.E. Div**   **}**   **76th Div**
>   **N. Army**   **89-90 Div.**
>   **Penn Div**   **28th**
>   **N.E. Div**   **26th**

S.R.O.T., Service Ranging Outpost Terrain, was the designation American troops gave to French observation outposts.

In the A.E.F. there were three distinct types of Army divisions, each filled in three completely different ways. The Regular Army Divisions, the 1st through the 8th, were manned by troops who were in the Regular Army when the war began. Because of the relatively small size of the Regular Army at this time, Congress authorized the immediate federalization of state National Guard units throughout the U.S. The newly-created divisions, the 26th through the 42nd, were designated as National Guard Divisions. Additional divisions were later generated through the draft. These divisions, the 76th through the 93rd, were referred to as National Army Divisions.

The 2nd Engineers were divisional troops assigned to the 2nd Division, Regular Army. The unit first saw combat at

Chateau-Thierry in June and July, 1918.

The 4th Marine Infantry Brigade was also attached to the 2nd Division. The 2nd Division arrived in France in October of 1917 along with the 26th, the 42nd, and the 1st Divisions. Members of these divisions referred to themselves as "The First Hundred Thousand."

The 41st Division was also known as the "Wildcat Division" because it was composed of guardsmen from states in the western part of the U.S.

The 42nd Division was often referred to as the "Rainbow Division" since its troops were selected from National Guard units from all across America.

Members of the 5th Division, a Regular Army division, wore the divisional red diamond patch on their shoulders. The 5th Division participated in both the Saint Mihiel and Meuse-Agonne Operations.

The 301st Infantry, 302nd Infantry and 303rd Infantry were assigned to the 151st and 152nd Infantry Brigades of the 76th Division, a National Army Division. The 76th was often called the "New England Division" since its troops were drafted from the states of Massachusetts, Connecticut, Maine, Rhode Island, New Hampshire, Vermont, and New York. The 76th Division saw action throughout the Lorraine sector.

The 89th and the 90th Divisions were both National Army Divisions. The 89th was organized at Fort Riley, Kansas and was composed of drafted personnel from the states of Arizona, Colorado, Kansas, Missouri, Nebraska, New Mexico, and South Dakota. The 90th was based at Fort Sam Houston, Texas and was made up of draftees from Texas and Oklahoma. Both divisions participated in the Saint Mihiel and Meuse-Argonne Operations.

The 28th Division came into existence when the entire Pennsylvania National Guard was federalized. The division engaged in combat at Chateau-Thierry, Champagne, Aisne, and in the Argonne.

National Guard units from the states of Connecticut, Maine, Massachusetts, New Hampshire, Rhode Island, and

Maine, Massachusetts, New Hampshire, Rhode Island, andVermont made up the 26th Division, also known as the "Yankee Division." The 26th was the first National Guard division to arrive in France in October of 1917. The division saw considerable action in the Champagne, Aisne, Saint Mihiel, and Argonne Operations.(11)

Major Williams F.A.   _Lt. Wright_
location of Big Bertha- Baubean Forest

First Lieutenant Jefferson D. Wright, Commerce, Georgia, was one of the first officers sent to the British front in 1917 to study Flash Ranging. He would later command Flash Ranging Section No. 2.(12)

The German 42cm Heavy Artillery Piece--"Big Bertha"

"Big Bertha" was a reference to a class of German heavy artillery. Designed to penetrate fortified concrete positions, the 420mm howitzer weighed 75 tons and required a crew of 200 men. Its great size dictated that it be transported by rail in five sections. "Big Bertha" could hurl a 2,200 lb. shell over nine miles. It was first used in 1914 during the German seige of Liege, Belgium. In describing the shelling his troops had to endure,

Belgian General Gerard Leman recalled the sound of rushing air that increased to a hurricane roar and concluded with a tremendous clap of thunder. Great geysers of dirt and smoke exploded into the air, and the earth below his feet rumbled. The 420mm guns were manufactured by the Krupp Works and were nicknamed after the daughter of Friedrich Alfred Krupp, Bertha Krupp von Bohlen und Halbach.(13)

Notes of Places
etc.

F.R.S. #3-Central-Crue.[Creue] *Annex*

    Crue [Creue]-*St. Morice* [St. Maurice]-*Heudicourt Dampvitoux*

    F.R.S. #2

    Thiacourt [Thiaucourt]-*Beney*

Oct. 10th-for-F.R.S. #2

    Approx. Line-Lachausse-Dampvitoux-Dommartin-Charey-Rembercourt-Mad Rv. Valley-Bois de Villacoy [Bois de Preny(Mon-Plaisir F me)

Preny (Mon-Plasir F me)

Bouwmont [Beaumont]	*-Base of Metz Drive*
Enverson [Enversin]	*-F.R.S. #2 Central*
Mammie [Mamey]	*- " #2 Before Drive*
Chaumont	*-G.H.Q.*
Buszy [Buzy]	*-lay over*
Essay [Essey]	*-A.I.S.H. 2.*
Nansaid [Nonsard]	
Mot Plasure Farm	
Pont a Mouson [Pont a Mousson]	

Flash Ranging Section #2 was organized in Langres on August 18, 1918. The unit included 15 experienced men from Flash Ranging Section #1. The troops had trained with French S.R.O.T. 88 and had participated in the Chateau-Thierry Operation. Rounding out the section were newly-trained men from Company C, 29th Engineers. F.R.S. #2 was commanded by

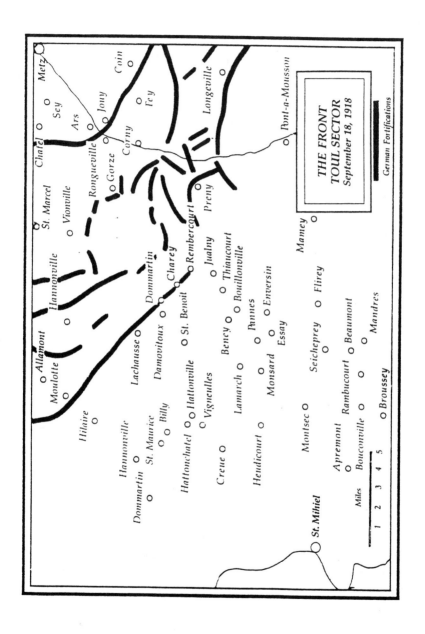

THE FRONT
TOUL SECTOR
September 18, 1918

German Fortifications

Lieutenant J.D. Wright and served in the Toul sector. Private Pfennig was transferred into this section from F.R.S. #3.(14)

Bois is the French word for woods.

Division Marks

1*st*	**Div.**	*1*
2*nd*	"	
3*rd*	"	
4*th*	"	
5*th*	"	◇ **Red**

The use of colored uniform patches as a means of identifying particular troops dates back to the American Civil War. The divisional shoulder sleeve insignia that is so commonly found on military unifroms today though dates back to 1918. The first unit to display such an insignia was the 81st Infantry Division, known to many as the Western or Wildcat Division. Members of the 81st preparing to embark for France from Hoboken, New Jersey, wore on their left shoulder a circular badge with a black "wild cat" affixed to its center. Other A.E.F. units in France eventually adopted their own distinctive patches. By the autumn of 1918, most American divisions had made the shoulder insignia an unofficial part of the uniform. Official permission to wear divisional emblcms was given on October 19, 1918.

In this entry, Private Pfennig attempted to draw in pencil the insignia patches for the first five American Army divisions. On the page he successfully sketched the emblems of the 1st, 2nd, and 5th Divisions. The 1st Division wore a large red figure "1." The 2nd Division chose a badge shaped like a shield. In the center of the patch was the head of an Indian Chief. The 5th

Division selected a simple red diamond as its distinguishing mark. Missing from the page are the insignia of the 3rd and 4th Divisions. The 3rd Division wore a square patch that had three diagonal stripes of white and blue. The white bars represented the divisional number. The blue bars had a two-fold meaning. Blue was the official color of the infantry. Blue also signified the blue waters of the Marne River. Since the 3rd Division did much of its fighting along this river in France, it was often called the "Marne Division." The 4th Division picked green ivy as its designated mark. On its badge, four clusters of green ivy were joined to make a diamond shape.(15)

Aeroplane Marks

Allied

Circle	*Red-White-Blue*	
Amer	*White Center*	
French	*Red*	*"*
British	*Blue*	*"*
Belgium	*Yellow*	*"*

Tails striped the same
M.G. used for signals streams.

When the U.S. entered the war in April of 1917, American aviation was backward compared to that of the combatants already engaged. The U.S. had only one squadron of airplanes and absolutely no accessory equipment. The 55 planes in the Aviation Section of the Signal Corps were obsolete and very, very slow. The most advanced American plane at the time, the Curtiss JN-4 Jenny, had a top speed of 75 miles per hour. By comparison, the Germans, the French, and the British possessed airplanes that were capable of flying 150 miles per hour or better. The U.S. had fewer than 50 trained pilots; none had combat experience with the exception of those who had volunteered to form the *Escadrille Americaine* within in the French Army. Lacking

as well was the basic, fundamental knowledge necessary to orga-
nize an air service. In essence, the U.S. had a lot of catching up
to do--quickly.

Initially, the American government, at the recommenda-
tion of the French, developed a grandiose plan to unleash the
productive power of the U.S. towards the construction of an air
force that could be fully operational for the 1918 campaigns. It
called for the production of over 20,000 planes and nearly 40,000
engines. These planes would be organized into 345 combat squadrons, 263 to be operational by June 1918. In addition, 45 construction companies, 81 supply squadrons, 11 repair squadrons,
and 26 balloon companies were planned. The price tag for this
ambitious project was $640,000,000, the largest amount ever
appropriated by Congress for a single purpose up to that time.

By the end of 1917, however, it was quite evident that the
U.S. would be unable to meet its first set of goals. A new study
was undertaken by members of the Aviation Section and the General Staff, and squadron figures were scaled back. The goal for
June 1918 was now 190 squadrons. A secondary mark of 270
squadrons was set for December of that same year. With reference to the production of airplanes in the U.S., it was decided
that expediance necessitated the use of French and British made
planes by American air squadrons. The U.S. would devote all of
its energies towards the manufacturing of an engine that would
be compatible with selected Allied planes. The engine, dubbed
the "Liberty," was eventually mated with the British-made
DeHavilland DH-4 light bomber.

The U.S. Air Service was organized around three basic
functions: observation, bombing, and fighter pursuit. Balloons
and airplanes were both useful as observation platforms. Observation and bombing missions were essentially carried out by the
same planes. The DeHavilland DH-4 and two French-made
planes, the Salmson 2A2 and the Breguet 14B2 were the three
most commonly used airplanes. All three were two-seater bi-
planes. The DH-4 was the only American-made plane to fly over
France during the war. Its tempermental dispostition and

tendency to break down earned the nickname "Flaming Coffin" from American pilots. The fighter aircraft used by the U.S. were built exclusively by the European allies. The French Nieuport 28 and the Spad S-13 and the British Sopwith F-1 Camel and the Royal Aircraft Factory's SE-5 were designed to intercept an attacking enemy with speed and manueverability.

Lieutenant Colonel William (Billy) Mitchell orchestrated the overhaul of the U.S. Air Service during World War I. Colonel Mitchell was the first American aviation officer sent to France to observe the air war. His recommendations to General Pershing and his General Staff provided the basis for the creation of a credible American air capability in Europe. While other officers later held the title Chief of Air Service and were responsible for the day-to-day operations of the air corps, Colonel Mitchell became the A.E.F.'s Tactical Air Commander in the Zone of Advance. He coordinated American air power during the Verdun, Saint-Mihiel, and Meuse-Argonne offensives.

At the time of the Armistice, there were 45 American air squadrons on the front line composed of 740 planes, nearly 800 pilots, and 500 observers. The following Air Service units of the U.S. Second Army were stationed at the front in the Toul sector near Private Pfennig's unit:

> 4th Corps Observation Group
> > 8th Corps Observation Squadron
> > 168th Corps Observation Squadron
> > 135th Corps Observation Squadron
>
> 6th Corps Observation Group
> > 354th Corps Observation Squadron
>
> 2nd Day Bombardment Group
> > 163d Day Bombardment Squadron

4th Pursuit Group
    141st Pursuit Squadron
    6th Air Park

4th Corps Balloon Group
    15th Balloon Group
    16th Balloon Group
    69th Balloon Company

6th Corps Balloon Group
    10th Balloon Company (16)

Colonel Billy Mitchell reviewing the 4th Pursuit Group, Air Service,
2nd Army

Soldiers of Germany

You ask Peace

> _A brute whose claws a dripping red_
> _Red blood our mothers hearts have shed!_
> _A fiend whose burned + smashed + torn_
> _The arts + creeds that Peace had born!_
> _Can pass the law of recompense_
> _For deeds like these._

"The Hun" as portrayed on a popular American war poster

In truth is power
> *And not in his can you efface*
> *The blot youve brought upon the race*
> *Save these your countrys while you may:*
> *Kingdoms like kings shall pass away.*
> *If they be held in evil thrall*
> *To play or conquer nations all*
> *This is your hour!*

Peace cannot be
> *Till Hunnish hate + H-lust*
> *Are buried in the smoulding dust*
> *That marks your passing Unde land.*
> *Peace harkens not to your demand*
> *Till all your vainglorious pride*
> *Has perished in the changeful tide*
> *Of destiny*

W. J. A.

A Prayer

Good Lord, deliver us from the hyphenated American, the pro-German, the spy, the profitier, the pacifist, the slacker and all who would retard the prosecution of the war for human right and human happiness in the establishment of a permanent world wide Peace for Christ sake.

Amen.

Rv. H.N. Condon

Only *a Volunteer*

Why didn't I wait to be drafted
And be led to the train by a band.
And put in a claim for exemption
Oh, why didn't I hold up my hand
Why didn't I wait for the banquet
Why didn't I wait to be cheered
For the drafted men get the credit
While I merely volunteered

And nobody gave me a banquet
And nobody said a kind word
The grind of the wheels of the engine
Was the only good by that I heard
Thou off to the camp I was hustled to be trained for
*   next half year*
And thou in the shuffle forgotten
I was only a volunteer

And maybe some day in the future
When my little boy sits on my knee
And asks what I did in the world war
And his little eyes look up to me
I will have to look back as I'm blushing
To eyes that so trustingly peer
And tell him I missed to be drafted
I was only a volunteer

                    Bristol Press
                    Stars + Stripes

The *Bristol Press* was Private Pfennig's hometown
newspaper. *Stars and Stripes* was the official newspaper of the
A. E. F. General Pershing was the force behind the newspaper's
creation. He believed a publication made available to the troops

would help to keep their morale high. The first issue of *Stars and Stripes* was distributed on February 18, 1918. By the time of the Armistice, its circulation had risen to over 500,000.(17)

Notes of Experience with F. R. S.
Left for Front
　　　Sept. 27th
　　　　　Sunshine-fair and cool　Worked won Barracks detail.　Notice to move at retreat at 8 A.M. all aboard. Marched to Langres station.　Slept in causal　Barracks on straw.　Some sleep.

　　　28
　　　Called at 3:30.　All aboard in III Class cars.　Went by way of Neufchateau and landed at Toul at 12:20.　Was served by Amer. Red Cross.　Went to Hd Qt's A. E. F. 29th Eng. Back of Toul Cathedral.　Went down town Neff-Cole-Myself visited French-Amer Bar for a royal good send off.　Ordered to salvage and turn in Barracks Bags.
　　　Route
　　　　　Langres-Bourmont-Neufchaeau-Toul

The Red Cross rest station at Toul, France

Carter H. Harrison, Captain in the American Red Cross provided a very detailed description of the city of Toul:

> In pre-war days, Toul had 14,000 inhabitants; a garrison of 40,000 had manned the ring of forts and bastions which,engirdling the city, made it second to Verdun among the fortressess of France. The same distance beyond the frontier, that Toul lay within, the Germans had made a like stronghold of Metz; with monster guns hidden on every hill and concealed in many a hollow, the giants had frowned at each other for four decades awaiting the inevitable conflict. The Moselle flows peacefully under the walls of each. In 1918 the civil population of Toul had shrunk to less than half its former numbers and French soldiers were few. Serving as headquarters of the 2nd Army of the AEF, its streets night and day were crowded with our khaki clad soldiers.
>
> That the city had been of medieval military importance is shown by the double walls and moats which hem it in; the walls are lichen hued, the moats green with rich grasses; the broad sweep forms a park, that is beautiful in the spring, when the centuries old maples and lindens shade the greensward and its winding walks. The perpendicular lower segment of the walls on the outside is of hewn stone; inward it is a gentle slope of turf covered earth. The distance from the moat floor to the height of the wall is great, as that of the nearby 4-storied buildings. Four gates pierce the wall; Three I took to be comparatively modern. Tunnel-like the _Porte de Metz_ burrows through the inner wall; on the moat side an old drawbridge and portcullis stand guard. The _Port de France_, the _Port de Nancy_ and most of all the _Porte Jeanne d'Arc_, if not opened in recent years, had been thoroughly brought to date; they were merely handsome roadways bisecting a park. Beyond the moat is the canal, a branch of the Meuse-Moselle waterway, which connects the rivers of France with the Rhine, a quiet water highway, lending itself naturally to the indolent life of bargemen and their families, for in the operation of a French canal-boat the family down to the children have their tasks. . . .
>
> Toul humble in size, its buildings insignificant, its streets crooked, dirty and ill paved, under the prevailing winter skies had a gray dinginess as its dominant color note. And yet for me it soon had a definite charm. It is a city with a soul. There is about it an indescribable something, which appeals directly to sentiment. What is lacking in architectural beauty is more than made good in the wealth of associations with tradition and history. . . .

The houses are commonplace; the winding steets might be termed alleys. The girding walls, built up on the inner side into two storied structures, before the war had been barracks, store houses, arsenals, powder magazines, stables, indeed housing for all the military needs of the troops, which had constituted its peace establishment. It was a city of little shops; barring the local department store of the *Credits Reunis* and a few mildly pretentious shops in the *rue Gambetta* and the *rue de la Republique*, its business was that of the boutique of the French interior, presided over by the good wife, whose husband goes to daily labors elsewhere.

The Tulum Leucorum of the Romans, Toul is one of the ancient towns of Lorraine; its bishopric was founded in the earliest of centuries of the Christian era by St. Mansuy, an Irish monk, who dying about the year A.D. 350, was buried in the fauburg named for him, in the vault of a chapel where the sarcophagus which once held his remains is preserved; his skull in the cathedral of St. Etienne is the city's holiest relic. Few are the wars fought by France which have not cast their shadows over Toul. Its great tragedy came in 1870-1871, when German might forced its fortress to yield. (18)

The headquarters of the 29th Engineers was located behind Toul's two-towered, Gothic cathedral, St. Etienne. The bar Private Pfennig noted in his diary was probably the Red Cross canteen, formerly known as the *Goutte de Cafe*, The Drop of Coffee:

The railroad canteen at Toul was operated by a woman in Red Cross uniform, with the aid of a staff of Red Cross girls. She had organized it on her own initiative, had built it up on her own courage, determination and energy, had made it a whale of a success; and she had force to pull against many currents. Miss Mary Vail Andress, when all is said and done, in this canteen and accessories, pulled off just about the biggest individual Red Cross stunt in the entire AEF, certainly in the American sector. From the small beginning of switching the French railroad canteen, the Goutte de Cafe, into an American canteen, there had grown by gradual degrees a great institution. The main building, formerly the Hotel de la Gare, with its canteen, rest room, writing room and reading quarters, was the four ring circus; its connected dormitories had beds for 400 enlisted men, and a system of hot shower baths, that served hundreds of boys a day. In the square fronting the station the Old Goutte de Cafe, greatly enlarged, was operated as a typical railroad canteen.(19)

Private Cole was later stationed at Outpost #1, F. R. S. #3. His particular skill as an observer was specifically mentioned in *Ranging in France With Flash and Sound*, a book that chronicles the World War I exploits of the 29th Engineers:

> This post [Post #1] was one of the satellites when it came to locating enemy batteries and reporting troop movments. The personnel of the post included one man, Private Cole, who held the place of honor in locating enemy planes.
>
> It is said that he could detect a plane from the time the aviator started his motor 30 kilometers behind the German line. Upon the aviator's arrival to within ten kilometers of the line, this specialist would jump from his seat, pour a pail of water on the fire, slip on his hobnailed shoes and prepare to count the men that followed him into the dugout. It was due to the strenuous efforts of Private Cole that a requsition was made to G.H.Q. for steam heat. The seclusiveness of this post enabled the linesmen to live in comfort. Their duties of kitchen police were only interfered with by an occasional souvenir hunt.(20)

29 Sunday

Rain+Sunshine-Cool Orders to make packs and be ready. Dinner 11:45 Autos ready at 1:30 P.M.-5 in Convoy. Lift passed up throu St. Mihiel Sector. Passed Mt. Sec. Reached quarters at 4:30 P.M. Took quarters at house previously occupied by officers. Some bunks and every thing. Every thing from running water water swimming pool bowling alley Theaters and cottages. Electric lights-latrines and hot water showers.

Pvt.   Geating-Rieger-Futcher-Weeks-Wicks-Quin+Church myself occupied room used by Lieut and Staff of Medical Detachment. Had desks, morris chairs, and spring bunks, stools etc. Sheet Iron stove. German papers and letters dated Sept 3d

Lieut Morrow, May+David in charge F.R.S. #3 (East of Crue [Creue]-So of vignuelles.)

Members of the 29th Engineers, F.R.S. #3:

>William J. Geating, Company D, Ashland, Pennsylvania

>Julius Rieger, Company D, Arlington, Rhode Island

>Arthur J. Futcher, Company D, Philadelphia, Pennsylvania

>William A. Weeks, Company D, Peekskill, New York

>Martin F. Quinn, Company E, Thomson, New York

>Lieutenant Sanford E. Church, Cleveland, Ohio

The trip to the front of F. R. S. Number 3 is described in detail by Sergeant Jesse R. Hinman, 29th Engineers:

>One day, about the first of October, a jubilent crowd of khaki-clad men squeezed their way out of a stuffy French coach and landed with their packs at the railway station in Toul. The men were from Company D, the latest graduates from the Flash Ranging School. Each with a vast amount of knowledge of the million different ways of locating enemy batteries, was bound for the front to put their theories into practice. After a night spent in Toul, the detachment, under the command of Lieutenants Hulings, May and David, were ordered to climb waiting trucks, which were to carry the men to their destination. The three hours' journey carried them to the shattered section in the region of the famous Mont Sec, from whose heights the Germans had looked down upon Allied armies for four years, and which were to later cause their disaster.

>An abrubt turn in the road led them down a little driveway, shaded on either side by an overhanging forest of huge oak trees, which the Hun had a short time before been using as camouflage to hide his troops' movements. The trucks slowed down and came to a stop at the end of the roadway. The men clambored out and fell into line, to be addressed by Lieutenant Perry, who was in command of the section. In a few short words the veteran lieutenant commanded:

>"Men, this is the front. Put on your tin hats and wear your gas masks at alert." The men fell out, produced their mess kits and

lined up for mess, consisting of "canned Willie and hard tack."

During the few days following their arrival, the men were busily engaged in attaining a thorough knowledge of the country from the French S. R. O. T. No. 88, which was waiting to be relieved by the Americans. The French were using a four post base that extended along the front for a distance of 10 kilometers. The sites for the posts were well chosen and suitably well located in the hills and woods commanding the territory occupied by the Germans between Metz and Conflans, including all the industrial centers in that area.

The buildings occupied by central were located in the Bois de Vigneulles and the location was formerly a German divisional headquarters. These were well constructed, and even included a shattered bath house, which was later repaired. Upon the arrival of the Flash Rangers, there was a wild scramble for billets, beds, stoves and tables. It was a very congenial bunch of men that made their home here, about the only arguments arising being over who cut the most wood, or who was to build the fire in the kitchen stove in the morning.(21)

Officers of the 29th Engineers, F. R. S. #3
> First Lieutenant Samuel R. Morrow, Carthage, Missouri
> Second Lieutenant Louis A. May, Columbia, South Carolina
> Second Lieutenant Joseph David, Muskegon, Michigan

30

Sunshine-cool Found most everything could be ask for. German helmets and ammunition all around. Took ride on narrow gauge rail. Gathered vegetables from German garden. No bombing during day but a royal send off at night. Aeroplane and a royal bombardment.

Good wishes for the future
Kind memories of the past
Remembrance in the present
And friendship to the last.

The narrow gauge railway was used behind the lines to transport ammunition, supplies, and even troops. The width of its track was approximately 20 inches. Since the track came in sections, a narrow gauge railway could be constructed very quickly onto virtually any terrain. The engines, although also built to a smaller scale, could still pull loads of over 10 tons. The narrow guage railway was operated by engineers under the auspices of the Light Railway Department.(22)

Nighttime aerial bombardment was a tactic often used by the Germans. Colonel William Mitchell, Chief of Air Service, 1st Army, commented very favorably on its effectiveness in his memoirs. The Germans used twin-engined planes capable of carrying up to two thousand pounds of bombs. In total, there were about 50 of these bombers on the front. A typical night operation employed four to eight planes dropping five or six hundred pound bombs. German day bombardment was not as advanced. A typical day raids were made by single, two-seater Rumpler aircraft. These photographic reconnaissance planes dropped small bombs weighing 15 to 20 pounds.(23)

Codes
Keg of Worms
Dinner Party
Warsaw-Hugnut

Post #2 F. R. S. #3--Bombardment at The Front--
Howe Post--Thiaucourt--Rumors of Peace--
Collapse of Central Powers

OCTOBER 1918

Oct. 1918

1. Bombardment lasted all night. Took walk down to Belcourt 1 kilo. Found German boots. Orders to move to post #2 F. R. S. #3-at French S. R. O. T. #88
Sgt. Draudt-Corps Burns-Pvt. Shine Meiger [Meagher]-*Fallon-Davis-Alman* [Allman] *Pvt Wolfinger Finan Put in for the night in German villa in "Villa Barbara" Had fine supper Cook Davis Pvt Wolfinger came out to take charge. Very quiet.*

A complete description of the four French S. R. O. T. #88 outposts taken over by F. R. S. #3 was given by Sergeant Hinman:

>   Observation post No. 1 was located nearly a kilometer behind central on a prominent hill above the village of Heudicourt. The post was some distance back of the lines, but its advantageous position enabled the observers to view the enemy's territory equally as well as well or better than in a balloon. Due to the ability of camouflage artists, the men or posts were never molested by stray shells. . . .
>   In the position which the French placed, Post No. 2 did not conform to the American plans. For a period of two weeks the observers struggled to perform their duties on the hill between Vigneulles and Heidicourt. A view of the enemy batteries in the region of Conflans could not be obtained owing to an interlying promotory on which was located the village of Hatton-Chatel, although very creditable work was accomplished by the observers in ranging and locating a battery in a barn in Souzmont. . . .
>   The men at this post were comfortably located in a small concrete house, which Fritz had previously constructed. This proved a very home-like abode and a controversy arose between the men and the French officers over who should occupy it, the observers finally coming to the conclusion that they did not 'parley Francais' and kept the billet. It was due to this fortunate circumstance that they retained their home.
>   A short time later a change in plans necessitated the moving of this post to the farthermost point in the section which was

near the front line.

No. 3 post was, perhaps, the best point of observation, being located in the east end of the village of Hatton-Chatel. The little hamlet could be seen from most any point for many miles, being located on one of the prominent heights of the Meuse.

One of the most interesting things noted from this post was the operating of a German naval rifle about eight kilometers back of the enemy lines. The Germans could be seen at work and the American observers could easily pick up the flash of the gun, which was often firing on Hatton Chatel. . . .

No. 4 post planted itself in the hills above the town of St. Maurice. It was hastily 'transplanted' on various occasions, due to some of Fritz's wandering barrages. In the early days of its existence the observers were braving the rains and doing their best to keep telephonic communication. Wet instruments and various other tributory causes made things very uncomfortable for the observers, but later a final and habitable post was established. The men who operated it were a credit to the section. (1)

Members of the 29th Engineers, F. R. S. #3:

    Walter A. Draudt, Company D, Columbus, Ohio

    Robert O. Burns, Company D, New Bedford, Massachusetts

    Manning T. Shine, Company D, Fulton, Alabama

    Thomas F. Meagher, Company D, Grindstone, Pennsylvania

    John D. Fallon, Company C, Uniontown, Pennsylvania

    Clyde M. Davis, Company B, Gardenville, Virginia

    Jack S. Allman, Company C, Fairbanks, Alaska

    Oliver R. Wolfinger, Company C, Seattle, Washington

    Joseph Finan, Company C, Lopez, Pennsylvania

Two weeks later, Post #2 was moved to a new location closer to the front. Cook Davis would later recall the first night of shelling he experienced on the front:

With the exception of machine gun fire, a few whizbangs and a little gas, the night was as calm as a June evening on the farm back home. Now wait--what I mean by a calm night, is when all this is happening at least a kilometer away from the observation post.

We were all draped around our bunks and there was a feeling of satisfaction and comfort prevalent, because this was the one time during the 24 hours when each lad could loosen his clothing, scratch cootie bites and catch the little fellows that scampered playfully around the middle of his back.

----Bang! Our worthy 'chef de poste' looked around and calmly announced that when we got ready to 'haul tail' for the dugout to kindly leave our blankets with him so he might sleep more comfortably. Just then another of Fritz's pets came over and hit much closer than the first. I knew it was much closer because 'chef de poste' drew a sharp breath, the petit corporal John Fallon dropped a cootie which he had just chased into the corner of his undershirt and captured by a flank movement. I didn't say anything, because I was buried deep beneath my blankets, and had my fingers crossed so that no shell fragments could touch me.

Now every story has its crisis--this one has one too. It came in the form of a long drawn out whine that ended in a full grown crash right in the middle of the billet next to our own. Now, I never did understand whether or not the 'chef' changed his mind, but he suddenly forgot all about borrowing any blankets. The only reason he got first place in the dugout was because he made better time than I getting there. It so happened that the mouth of the 'safety cellar' had been tightly boarded up and a stove placed before it. I do not know how the obstruction was removed, but I passed the stove in mid air. Up to this time everything had worked as if planned, but it was found that the 'chef de poste' was small, but the opening smaller. Nevertheless, the chef passed through. I was not so fortunate. Due to an expanded waist band, caused no doubt by my fondness for monkey meat, that my companions declined, I stuck fast. However, the monkey in the meat appeared to be of much assistance to me at this time for I felt myself much more agile. By twisting and squirming I managed to get inside.(2)

2. Cool all day went out to ap. #2 Looked country over. Barrage opened at 4:30 A. M. by Amex. Was a heavy one Closed at 7:-- German 155 hammered away at   all afternoon. Austrian   Bang-Wiz-Bang 88

The word *barrage* was borrowed from the French by both English and American armies. In common speech, it is defined as either a turnpike barrier or a dam. A more literal meaning is preventing movement. It was the latter definition that was adopted by the French military. The *tir de barrage* was the blanket of exploding shells that shielded advancing infantry from attack by the enemy. In theory, the barrage pinned enemy infantry down in defensive shelters until it was too late to mount a credible defense against the attacking forces.

In *The Artilleryman*, Jay M. Lee of the 129th Field Artillery gives a brief and yet thorough explanation of the artillery barrage:

> Artillery fire by a considerable number of guns so directed that the shells fall and burst in an extended line, usually where the enemy infantry is advancing or threatening to advance, or are in position where it is desired to overwhelm or drive them back.
>
> A creeping or rolling barrage is one where the range is gradually increased in short successive increments, by all guns uniformly, so that the effect is to clear the field of enemy troops in front of our advancing infantry.
>
> When the barrage is continued on one line without changing the range it is called a standing barrage, or curtain of fire.
>
> When a barrage is laid directly in front of our own lines to secure it against an enemy advance it is called a protective barrage.

(3)

The German 155mm heavy howitzer

In the early stages of World War I, when mobile operations were still a possibilty, the artillery piece of choice of all major combatants was the light field gun. For the French, it was the 75mm M-1897; for the Germans, it was the 77mm C96 n/A. Tactics and weaponry later changed when a stalemate developed along a 475 mile front. Siege warfare necessitated heavier ordnance, and the Germans initially had an advantage in this area. By 1918, of the 20,000 artillery pieces in the German army, nearly 8,000 were heavy guns. At the corps level, German troops were bolstered by batteries of 155mm heavy howitzers. (4)

The "Austrian 88" cited by Private Pfennig most likely refers to the Austrian-made 88mm cannon. Allied soldiers did not soon forget the sound of a barrage laid down by this artillery piece. The narrations of other Flash Rangers describing the flight and detonation of an 88mm shell are identical to Private Pfennig's. All recount the particular sounds "Wiz-Bang" of incoming 88's. (5)

3. Very quiet except for a few German 155 sent over into Crue [Creue]. *Quite a few Aero-planes going over head. F. R. S. #3 started to take ahold of posts.*

4. Cool and clear. Went on watch for six hours from 6 A.M. to 12 M. Some big boys came over. I was "compris" and respect them. Crue [Creue] *caught hell was on post from 6 AM 12 M. Trimble brothers joined out fit.*

Compris is a French adjective defined as understood or included.

The Trimble brothers of the 29th Engineers:
Chester B. and Lowell D., Company C, Idaho
Falls, Idaho

5. *Cool and clear-very foggy. F. R. S. #3 took over
S. R. O. T. 88 at 10 A. M. Was on post from 7 A. M. -19. A
very quiet day. Nothing much doing all around. Watches
changed time.*

6. <u>*Sunday*</u>
Very quiet all day except for a few in V--+ St.M.
[Vigneulles and St. Maurice] *Ballon went up and six
aeroplanes came over with a dip the dip and down she came.
Hayward joined party. Meager* [**Meagher**] *left. Went on
watch at 19 oclock-Twice changed-one hour at 12 M. Re-
ceived some lovely letters dated Sept 9th latest. Note from
Julius from hospital in England. Night very quiet. Notice of
German Austro Peace proposals.*

An Allied observation balloon under enemy attack

Both the Allies and the Germans used observation balloons throughout World War I. In 1918 alone, one might be able
to spot as many as 300 balloons, both Allied and German, strung
up at various points along the front.The French were the prime
suppliers of kite balloons for the Allied side.Nearly 4,000 Caquots,
as they were called, were produced over the span of the war. The
sausage-shaped Caquot held 1,000 cubic meters of hydrogen and

carried an observer up nearly 5,000 feet. The German counter-
part to the Caquot was the Drachen. Phallic-shaped, the Drachen
was dubbed *"das Madchens Traum,"* the maiden's dream--for
obvious reasons.

Observers in balloons had a number of advantages over
their counterparts in airplanes. At 4,000 feet on a clear day, the
balloon observer could see nearly 15 miles beyond the enemy's
front lines. The use of balloons allowed data collection over a
longer period of time, from dawn to dusk if need be, and constant
communication with the ground through a direct telephone line
was always possible. When balloons were assigned to attacking
forces, effects of preliminary barrages were measured, the strength
of enemy defenses gauged, and the progress of advancing infantry units determined. Along a static front, balloons were just as
useful. High powered binoculars enabled spotters to plot enemy
movement on the rails and on the roads. Airborne observers also
were able to use still photography. Oblique photographs of enemy positions taken high above at various intervals along the
front could be spliced together to provide panoramic views of
the enemy's entire defensive alignment.

Perhaps the most important role played by balloon observers along the front was related to artillery spotting. The artillery technology which evolved during World War I allowed guns
to hit targets far beyond the range of human eyesight on the
ground. For the first time in history, artillery batteries almost
never saw their targets. It was this combination of increased firepower and aerial observation by balloon that made the artillery
piece the most important weapon of the war.

The downing of a balloon as described in Private Pfennig's
entry was not an uncommon sight. Both weather and enemy fire
took their toll on balloons and observers alike. The average
lifespan of a kite balloon operating in an active sector of the western front was about 15 days. All told, the A. E. F. lost 100 balloons on the front, 65 to enemy attack and 35 to natural wear and
tear. Following the war, it was discovered that the German
system of rating aviators ranked the downing of a balloon equal

to one and one-half planes. Such was the respect the German general staff had for the work of the Allied kite balloons. Observers caught in the cupola of a hydrogen balloon under attack from enemy airplanes or enemy artillery undoubtedly endured a terrifying experience. Ignition of the hydrogen gas was always a threat. Since arming the observers themselves proved to be impractical, antiaircraft units were usually given the duty of protecting the balloons. As an added safety precaution, every balloon observer was required to be harnessed to a parachute already suspended within the balloon. (These French-made parachutes had a reputation of not opening cleanly.) But parachuting cleanly out of a burning balloon filled with 20,000 cubic feet of hydrogen was a feat easier said than done. Most balloon observers used the parachute as an extreme last resort. (6)

Members of the 29th Engineers:
Don M. Hayward, Company C, Kenne, New
Hampshire
Thomas F. Meagher, Company D, Grindstone,
Pennsylvania
Julius Rieger, Company D, Arlington, Rhode
Island

In the final days of September, a panic-stricken German High Command concluded that eventual defeat was a definite certainty. This realization caused particular shock and confusion within Germany's government, a government which had never contemplated any other outcome but victory. On September 29, Germany's two top military commanders General Eric Ludendorff and Field Marshal Paul Von Hidenburg implored Kaiser Wilhelm II to immediately sue for peace under the terms of President Woodrow Wilson's Fourteen Points. The Kaiser sadly concurred with his commanders' advice and set into motion a series of actions intended to give President Wilson the impression that Germany was indeed sincerely ready to agree to an armistice. On October 1, Chancellor George Von Hertling's government was forced to resign. One day later, Kaiser Wilhelm appointed to the chancellorship the most liberal royalist in the German empire, Prince Maximilian of Baden, and as a final sign of his intent to usher in a more popular government in Germany, the Kaiser signed a proclamation surrendering some of his powers.(7)

7 Cool and Rainy Transfered from Post #2 F R S #3 to Howe Post F. R. S. #2 Located east of Thucourt [Thiaucourt]. *German Guns very quiet all day. Andrews-Bensen* [Bentzen]- *Neff and Wilconx also sent to F. R. S. #2 Papers give space to peace proposals. Report Kaiser dead. " Did you hear what happened to the Crown Prince?"*

Lieut Wright-C. O. of F. R. S. #2

F. R. S. #2 was positioned near Mon Plasir Farm, The area was under constant machine gun fire from the Germans.

Flash Ranging Section #2 had four observation posts. Each was named after a sergeant in the unit. Howe Post was named after Sergeant George B. Howe, Company D, Portland, Oregon. Cotton Post, Brewster Post, and Chambers Post were the other three outposts.(8)

Another view from Mon Plasir Farm showing Bois de Dommartin
in the distance

Members of the 29th Engineers:

> Robert M. Andrews, Company D, Harrisburg,
>   Pennsylvania
> Aage C. Bentzen, Company C, Manchester,
>   New Hampshire
> Harold E. Neff, Company D, Sunburg,
>   Pennsylvania
> Fred B. Wilcox, Company C, Parishville, New
>   York

> **8**   ***Cool and Rainy. Very quiet all day. Allied***
> ***batteries active. Boche moving around with packs. More***
> ***space to Peace. The big word of the world. Neff went on***
> ***Howe post for the day. 24 hours on 48 off.***
>   ***Read our sea mail Sept 12***
>   ***Sent German Helmet to R--.***
>   ***What happened to our billet. Located in death valley***
> ***east of death curve.***

The French word *Boche* is a slang term which refers to a
bloody revolutionist or a German. According to the 1943 edition of *Funk and Wagnalls New Standard Dictionary of the*

English Language, the exact origin of the word Boche is unknown. It was perhaps derived from the name of a Parisian butcher and revolutionary leader, Simon Caboche. Caboche was notorious for the atrocities he committed in 15th century France.

A view of "Death Valley" taken from Rembercourt Ridge.

"Dead Man's Curve" was a stretch of road located between the towns of Mandres and Beaumont. This notorious piece of highway was known to all including those in the Salvation Army:

> . . .The enemy's eye was always upon it and had its range.
> Before the St. Mihiel drive one could go to Bouconville or Raulecourt only at night. As soon as it was dark the supply outfits on the trucks would be lined up awaiting the word from the Military Police to go.
> Everyone had to travel a hundred yards apart. Only three men would be allowed to go at once, so dangerous was the trip. . . . The ride through the night in the dark without lights, without sound, over rough, shell-plowed roads had plenty of excitement.(9)

9 Cool but clear Fritz came back strong after day of rest but Sammy was ready to reply. Aeroplanes very active. Fritz played with 130 and 155 on all sides of us. Was on Howe post for the day. 89 Div moved into section. Frost and ice for first time. Robb's post got supreme piss shelled out of them and handed ass. Dodged 88s.

When the first American troops arrived in France, they were called "Sammies," after Uncle Sam. The name never became popular with the majority of soldiers. Most Americans preferred to be called "Doughboys" or "Yanks."(10)

The German 130mm Field Gun could send an 89 lb. shell to a target nearly nine miles away.(11)

Member of the 29th Engineers:
James M. Robb, Company C, Delaware County, Pennsylvania

10   Clear and cool. Hun batteries busy all day 150-210 a specialty went on a sheet salvaging tour at Thiaucourt. Aero planes very active. 5 Hun vs 3 Allied and one allied plane downed in flames
Battery shelling Thiaucourt situated at Metz 210 known by F, R, S, #2 as Thiaucourt Special

The results of German bombardment in Thiaucourt, October 3, 1918.

The Huns were a nomadic, warlike people from Central Asia. Under the leadership of Attila, the Huns overran much of central and eastern Europe by A. D. 450. In the early 20th century, German soldiers were often referred to as Huns. Apparently this designation was coined by Kaiser Wilhelm II himself. The 1943 edition of *Funk and Wagnalls New Standard Dictionary of the English Language* claims the Kaiser exhorted German troops bound for China to fight like the Huns of Attila. The speech was delivered on July 26, 1900 at Bremerhaven. During World War I, Allied soldiers used the term Hun to desribe German soldiers in a disparaging manner.

The German 150mm Field Howitzer

The German 210mm Howitzer

Each German corps contained a minimum of 12 150mm heavy howitzers. Capable of firing a 100 lb. shell a distance of five miles, these big guns were known for their noisy, black smoke explosions. German troops nicknamed them "Jack Johnsons" after the black world heavyweight boxing champion of 1908 to 1915.

The 210mm Mortar was another German heavy artillery piece. A 210mm Mortar could launch a 185 lb. projectile over five miles.(12)

World War I records do not give a very accurate account of the actual number of aircraft destroyed in combat. From the Allied perspective, the accounting of downed German aircraft was very imprecise at best. Like the Air Services of Great Britain and France, the U. S. Air Service used a "victory system" to acknowledge the downing of enemy aircraft. _USAF Historical Study no. 133, U. S. Air Service Victory Credits, World War I_ outlined the problems inherent in each of the victory systems:

> . . . official credit for a victory won in aerial combat could be awarded to an aviator of the A. E. F. if any aircraft was destroyed over enemy territory or fell or landed within an area held by the U. S. or allied forces. No credit could be awarded for an enemy aircraft that was forced down but made a normal landing in enemy territory. In practice these rules, in which the term "aircraft" included both airplanes and balloons, were expanded to give credit for destruction of balloons inflated in their beds on the ground.
> . . . The British divided credits so that each person who contributed directly to a victory received an equal fraction of the credit. The French and Americans, however, awarded a full credit to each person who contributed to a victory. Under the latter system, if two pilots in monoplace pursuit planes brought down an enemy aircraft, each pilot received one credit. If either the pilot or observer in a biplane airplane shot down an enemy aircraft, each received one credit, which resulted in credits for persons who, in fact did not shoot any enemy aircraft. Furthermore, the credits became rather complicated when several pilot-observer teams were involved in one victory. In two cases, sixteen men (eight pilots and their observers)

were each given one credit for the enemy airplane they all helped
to bring down.

Given such accounting methods, it is not surprising then
that Allied victory counts exceeded actual German losses. The
Allies claimed 11,760 air victories: 7,054 British; 3,950 French;
and 756 American. Postwar German calculations noted approximately 3,000 planes lost in battle on the Western Front. German
claims on Allied losses contained similar although smaller dis-
crepancies. According to American records, it would be safe to
say that in seven months of aerial warfare the A. E. F. Air Service
lost nearly 300 planes.(13)

**11   Cloudy + cool. frost each morning. Slept on
sheets. Salvaged a couple of horses from the French Artilary.
Things very quiet all day. Fritz only got excited once.**
Post got royal piss shelled out of it.
Occurances need not be noted
Ranged and shot up Main St. in Thiaucourt.

World War I ushered in a number of technological ad-
vances in warfare--the airplane, the tank, poison gas, and the
machine gun. In the field of transportation, however, both the
Allies and the Central Powers depended on a very ancient
mode--the horse. During World War I, the U.S. employed tens of
thousands of horses and mules to cart supplies, ammunition, and
artillery pieces. The fact that the A. E. F. was continually short of
horses might explain why Private Pfennig chose to acknowledge
his salvage of two horses from the French. General Pershing
noted numerous times in his memoirs the problems American
units had in acquiring horses for transportation purposes:

> The horse question was one that gave us trouble
> continuously. On account of the lack of shipping and the scarcity of
> forage in France,and in view of the promise of the French to
> purchase and deliver to us 15,000 animals per month from April to
> August, both inclusive, we had, in March, recommended to the War

Department that shipments from home be discontinued. But, as has been stated, the French farmers were reluctant to sell animals, even at the increased prices offered, and the climax came on May 31st, when the French advised that due to military developments on the Western Front the Government had issued orders suspending the purchase of any additional animals for the American forces.

I immediately took the matter up with M. Tardieu, of the Franco-American Committee, calling his attention to the extent to which the French failure to supply animals would immobilize a considerable portion of our forces. As a result, the French agreed to adopt a system of enforced requisition throughout France, commencing on June 20th and extending to August 1st. It was estimated that there were in France not in military service approximately 3,000,000 animals, of which 300,000 to 400,000 were thought to be suitable types. We were promised 80,000 of the 160,000 to be obtained through the requisition and in addition counted on approximately 14,000 from the British, in accordance with their promise to supply horses for the divisions behind their lines. . . .

From my conference with Foch and from M. Tardieu's cablegram, it was apparent that we could expect no assistance from the French after the 80,000 requisitioned horses had been delivered and that there must be a large increase in the number to be shipped from home, which we had been trying to avoid. Making every allowance for the possiblity of substituting motor traction for horses, still we should need for the 80-division plan something over 200,000 or 25,000 a month for the following eight months, a number that seemed prohibitive in view of the already enormous tonnage required for everything else. These numbers were never reached and we were always approximately 50 per cent short of our requirements. The question continued to give us concern to the end.

Indeed, it did. In November of 1918, Sergeant Howard Fisher of the 306th Field Artillery, 77th Division complained his unit's biggest problem involved the few horses they had left. Most were skin and bones. Had the war continued much longer, he feared they would have had to resort to pulling the 75's by hand.(14)

12 Cool and clear. Went on post at 8 A.M. Not much doing all day. 3 balloons put during afternoon. Dark at 5:30. Activity started in early. Troops ready for front. Germans throw over 30 minute barrage of 88-105-155 gas and H. E. Exciting night dirt flew in o. p. [Outpost] **Guns objective the moon. Run out of batteries. Salvaged two horses of French. Slept in sheets and pajamas.**

A German 105mm Light Field Howitzer

The 105m light field howitzer 98/09 was the most common German field howitzer deployed in World War I. The artillery piece fired 28 lb. shells at a velocity of 1,083 feet per second. It had a range of four miles.(15)

The Germans used a number of substances in their gas shells. Gas projectiles were marked with colored crosses that symbolized the particular chemical agent inside. British Intelligence described the various German munitions in a handbook designed for Allied troop use:

> "Green Cross" contains diphosgene (trichlormethychloroformate), a liquid with an unpleasant smell resembling phosgene. It is highly lethal and slightly lachrymatory [causing tears], but has little persistence.

> "Green Cross 1" contains diphosgene mixed with chloropicrin, the vapour of which has a powerful lachrymatory effect, and is also lethal. This filling is more persistent than the preceeding one. Recent specimens of this filling contain a red dye which has no toxic properties. It stains the shell holes so that they may be easily identified.

"Green Cross 2" contains phosgene, diphosgene and diphenylchlorasine. The latter substance is a solid. Small quantities of its vapour cause pain in the nose and throat, and sneezing. The mixture is lethal and lachrymatory, but has only slight persistence.

"Blue Cross"--In this type about two-thirds of the shell is filled with H.E., the remaining spaces being occupied by a glass bottle containing diphenylchlorasine. The shell bursts with an explosion similar to that of an ordinary H.E. shell and causes sneezing. It is often used with one of the types of "Green Cross" shell described above.

       In a projector bomb of recent introduction, the H.E. and diphenylchlorasine form one substance, made up in the form of pellets about the size of a pea. This substance detonates readily, producing a black smoke which is extremely irritant to the respiratory organs.

"Yellow Cross" contains dichlorethylsulphide, the so-called "mustard gas," a liquid with a faint garlic-like smell. Although the vapour produces no immediate discomfort, it is highly lethal, and, in addition, produces inflammation some hours after exposure. If the skin comes in contact with the liquid or is exposed to the concentrated vapour, no pain is felt at the time, but blisters are developed about six hours afterwards.

       Dichlorethylsuphide is very persistent and may remain in the ground for several days after a bombardment.

       A variation of "Yellow Cross" (possibly "Yellow Cross 1") consists of about equal parts of ethyldichlorasine and dichlormethyleter. This is a liquid, brown in colour, tranparent and fuming rather strongly in air.

       It has a pungent smell described variously as like chloroform and like garlic. The physiological effects are irritation of the eyes, nose and throat, sneezing, headache, vomiting, and loss of feeling in the hands and feet. The last-mentioned symptom is the most characteristic, and is due to the ethyldichlorasine.

       This gas dissipates more rapidly than the original "Yellow Cross"

H. E. was the abbreviation for High Explosive. The H. E. shell was designed to kill its targets through an initial blast explosive. Secondary casualties occurred when the steel casing of of the projectile shattered into fine splinters. Most German H. E. shells contained a mixture of trinitrotoluene (T.N.T.) and ammonium nitrate.(16)

> **13   Sunday**
> *Cloudy and cool Very quiet except for a few high burst range-5th Div. move up. 37th Eng. Div. back from Argon Woods* [Argonne Forest].
> *2 P.M.-A. I. S. wire reported German acceptance of Wilson's proposals. Dark nights at 6 oclock*
> **18   "**

The 37th Engineers was an electrical and mechanical regiment assigned to the U. S. Second Army.

On October 3, the German Imperial Chancellor Max of Baden drafted a note requesting an armistice. The note was passed through the Swiss and delivered to President Wilson on October 4. It read:

> The German Government requests the President of the United States of America to take steps for the restoration of peace, to notify all belligerents of this request, and to invite them to delegate plenipotentiaries for the purpose of taking up negotiations. The German Government accepts, as a basis for the peace negotiations, the program laid down by the President of the United States in his message to Congress of January 8, 1918, and in his subsequent pronouncements, particularly in his address of September 27, 1918. In order to avoid further bloodshed the German Government requests to bring about the immediate conclusion of a general armistice on land, on water, and in the air.

President Wilson received a similar note from the Austro-Hungarian government on the very same day.

President Wilson did not immediately reply to this first German note. Instead, he chose to ponder the German appeal privately for four days. Oddly enough, during this period of contemplation, Wilson neglected to notify the other Allies. The leaders of France, Italy, and Great Britain were not informed of the German cable nor were they consulted when Wilson finally drafted a response to it. (Ironically, on October 7, Premiers Clemenceau, Orlando, and Lloyd George were secretly meeting to discuss how they could head off implementation of Wilson's Fourteen Points.) Wilson's rejoinder, drafted by Secretary of State Robert Lansing, was cabled to the Germans on October 8 through the Swiss. The message deliberately avoided answering Germany's request for an armistice. Instead, it demanded from the Germans greater clarification on a number of issues contained in their initial cable:

> Before making a reply to the request of the Imperial German Government, and in order that the reply shall be as candid and straightforward as the momentous interests involved require, the President of the United States deems it necessary to assure himself of the exact meaning of the Note of the Imperial Chancellor. Does the Imperial Chancellor mean that the Imperial German Government accepts the terms laid down by the President in his address to the Congress of the United States on the 8th of January last and in subsequent addresses and that its object in entering into discussions would be only to agree upon the practical details of their application?
>
> The President feels bound to say, with regard to the suggestion of an armistice, that he would not feel at liberty to propose a cessation of arms to the Governments with which the Government of the United States is associated against the Central Powers so long as the Armies of those Powers are upon their soil. The good faith of any discussion would manifestly depend upon the consent of the Central Powers immediately to withdraw their forces everywhere from invaded territory.
>
> The President also feels justified in asking whether the Imperial Chancellor is speaking merely for the constituted authorities of the Empire who have so far conducted the war. He deems the answers to the questions vital from every point of view.(17)

14   Clear + cool Rumored that Artilary was to fire on the 15th only when fired on. And oh boy I guess then our Artilary was afraid they would have to carry back. Extra German activity all around but oh my.

*15   Rain + cool Wilson turns and picks an "if" in
Boch proposal. Our artlary let go all day. 75-90-105 moved in
al around. Very exciting. Sent over a message in shells. Heavy
barrage thrown over east of Verdun heard from our sector.*
        Surrender or get out under our fire.
        *Sent 2 helmets out by truck. 155's made use a call
looking for our batteries.*

Augmenting the 75mm field artillery piece, the A. E. F.
used a French-made 90mm field gun and a 105mm field gun.
The 90mm cannon could fire an 18 lb. shell over six miles. The
105mm field piece was capable of sending a 35 lb. projectile
over eight miles.(18)

*16   Cloudy-Rain-Cool Things very quiet during day.
Artilary moving in. Infantry divisions changing and Fritz found
it out and landed a few. One line went out and while fixing
over came a 210 singing along a two inch ditch seemed a yard.
Out side of that nothing doing. Thiaucourt came over from
Metz.*

*18 17 Rain-Cloudy+cool. Mud. Very quiet except at
times. Nothing doing. Our artilary was moving in daily some
good ones alright.*
        Turned in information on moving in and let have go

*17 18 Clear and cool Went on post 8 A. M. Artilary
opened up all day. Noisy night. At morning opened up with
H. E. and gas and gas came in o.p. I got a good mess of tear
and snizz. Nothing else doing. Orders issued to be ready to
pull and go ahead. eighteen aero planes at it in after noon.
One came down in flames.*

American troops often used the term "snizz" to describe
gas munitions that caused inflammation of the nasal passages
and sneezing.

19   *Rain+cool Got issue of under wear size 38.*
Things very quiet during day. Our batteries opened up at
night
"All for hell-Hoboken-Heaven by Christmas," Gen.
Pershing. Battery of U.S. 210 moved in front of us. Battery
of 90's only set in this sector operating to the rear. Got
Gasses for first time.
Americans gained 12 miles on 31 mile front in the
Argon [Argonne].
Austria divided into four states and left Germany is
report over A. I. S. German sent new note to Wilson.

From April 6, 1917 to November 11, 1918, the U.S.
shipped a monumental supply of clothing and equipment overseas to the American Expeditionary Forces. Private Pfennig's
new underwear was one of 14,701,000 pairs of summer and winter drawers distributed overseas to American servicemen. Other
items sent to U.S. troops abroad included 3,127,000 blankets;
9,074,000 coats; 6,401,000 flannel shirts; 6,191,000 wool trou-
sers; 9,136,000 marching and field shoes; 29,733,000 wool socks;
15,693,000 summer and winter undershirts.(19)

The Meuse-Argonne Operation evolved into the most
prolonged battle in U.S. history and the last major Allied effort
of World War I. Lasting 47 days, the engagement utilized over
1,200,000 troops. Elements of the French 4th Army and the U.S.
1st Army initiated the attack on September 26 along a 24 mile
front. Gradually, the attacking front was widened until it extended
from the Argonne Forest to the Moselle River, a distance of 90
miles. Movement in this wilderness region was particularly difficult; fighting was exceptionally fierce. Heavily equipped German forces dug in along the Hindenburg Line put up stiff resistance throughout the battle. The Argonne Operation was termi-
nated with the signing of the Armistice on November 11. While
American forces had driven the German line back 32 miles north-

ward and 14 miles to the northeast, they had also incurred 117,000 casualties in the process.(20)

On October 14, the German government sent a second note via the Swiss Foreign Office to President Wilson. The communication attempted to put to rest any questions regarding Germany's acceptance of the Fourteen Points and the desire to leave occupied territory. It also specifically noted that the authority of the German government flowed from the Reichstag and the German people and not the Emperor:

> In reply to the question of the President of the United States of America the German government hereby declares:
> The German Government has accepted the terms laid down by President Wilson in his address of January 8 and in his subsequent addresses as the foundations of a permanent peace of justice. Consequently its object in entering into discussions would be only to agree upon practical details of the application of these terms.
> The German Government believes that the Governments of the powers associated with the United States also accept the position taken by President Wilson in his addresses.
> The German Government in accordance with the Austro-Hungarian Government for the purpose of bringing about an armistice declares itself ready to comply with the propositions of the President in regard to evacuation.
> The German Government suggests that the President may occasion the meeting of a mixed commission for making the necessary arrangements concerning the exacuation.
> The present German Government which has undertaken the responsibility for this step towards peace has been formed by conferences and in agreement with the great majority of the Reichstag. The Chancellor, supported in all of his actions by the will of this majority, speaks in the name of the German Government and of the German people.

President Wilson drafted an immediate reply to the second German note on October 14--again without consultation with Allied leaders. Secretary of State Lansing delivered it to the Swiss Charge in Washington. The harsh language of this cable differed considerably from the conciliatory spirit of President Wilson's previous communications. The reasons for this change in tone can partially be attributed to a rash of untimely German submarine attacks on Allied passenger ships in the Atlantic. (The Japanese liner _Hiramo Maru_ was sunk off the Irish coast with the loss of 292 lives on October 4. The British mail boat _Leinster_ was torpedoed twice in the Irish Channel six days later. An additional 527 lives, including those of many women and children, were lost.) President Wilson was also under fire from the Republican Party for appearing to be too soft on the Central Powers. With a presidential election at hand, President Wilson undoubtedly succumbed to political pressure to act in a more bellicose manner towards the Germans.

President Wilson's second communique displayed two significant shifts in American thought regarding an armistice. First, he asserted that it would be up to the military leaders to broker an armistice--an armistice which by Wilson's definition had to guarantee the military superiority of U. S. and Allied forces on the ground in Europe. Second, President Wilson in no uncertain terms demanded the removal of Kaiser Wilhelm II from power in Germany as a prerequisite for peace. If Germany ever had thoughts of exiting the World War with some semblance of honor-- as an equal with her enemies--those thoughts were dashed on October 14:

> The unqualified acceptance by the German Government and by a large majority of the German Reichstag of the terms laid down by the President of the United States of America in his address to the Congress of the United States on the 8th of January, 1918, and in his subsequent addresses, justifies the President in making a frank and direct statement of his decision with regard to the communications of the German Government of the 8th [6th] and 12th of October, 1918.
>
> It must be clearly understood that the process of evacuation and the conditions of an armistice are matters which must be left to the judgement and advice of the military advisers of the Government of the United States and the Allied Governments, and the President feels it his duty to say that no arrangements can be accepted by the

the Government of the United States which does not provide absolutely satisfactory safeguards and guarantees of the maintenance of the present military supremacy of the armies of the United States and of the Allies in the field. He feels confident that he can safely assume that this will also be the judgement and decision of the Allied Governments.

The President feels that it is also his duty to add that neither the Government of the United States nor, he is quite sure, the Governments with which the Government of the United States is associated as a belligerent will consent to consider an armistice so long as the armed forces of Germany continue the illegal and inhumane practices which they still persist in. At the very time that the German Government approaches the Government of the United States with proposals of peace its submarines are engaged in sinking passenger ships at sea, and not the ships alone but the very boats in which their passengers and crews seek to make their way to safety; and in their present enforced withdrawl from Flanders and France the German armies are pursuing a course of wanton destruction which has always been regarded as in direct violation of the rules and practices of civilized warfare. Cities and villages, if not destroyed, are being stripped of all they contain not only but often of their very inhabitants. The nations associated against Germany cannot be expected to agree to a cessation of arms while acts of inhumanity, spoilation, and desolation are being continued which they justly look upon with horror and with burning hearts.

It is necessary, also, in order that there may be no possibility of misunderstanding, that the President should very solemnly call the attention of the Government of Germany to the language and plain intent of one of the terms of peace which the German Government has now accepted. It is contained in the address of the President delivered at Mount Vernon on the Fourth of July last. It is as follows: "The destruction of every arbitrary power anywhere that can separately, secretly, and of its single choice disturb the peace of the world; or, if it cannot be presently destroyed, at least its reduction to virtual impotency." The power which has hitherto controlled the German Nation is of the sort here described. It is within the choice of the German Nation to alter it. The President's words just quoted naturally constitute a condition precedent to peace, if peace is to come by the action of the German people themselves. The President feels bound to say that the whole process of peace will, in his judgement, depend upon the definiteness and the satisfactory character of the guarantees which can be given in this fundamental matter. It is indispensable that the Governments associated against Germany should know beyond a peradventure with whom they are dealing.

The President will make a separate reply to the Royal and Imperial Government of Austria-Hungary.(21)

20 Sunday   Clear but cool   Nothing exciting. Our guns did a little Ranging. Huns throw over a few bracketing o.p.   89th-90th Div, in rest at rear. Aero planes very active all around. Read Mail

21 Clear and cool. Aero planes and ballons very active. Went on duty 8 A. M. for 24 hours. nothing special except big guns   20:00 oclock Germans bombed Thiaucourt-Engineers dump   Our barrage opened at 21:00 oclock. Lasted some 35 minutes 75-210 used. Opened again later on

Thiaucourt under fire.

22   3:
       Clear and cool   3:20 Our barrage opened up again and men went over the top. Got information and 41 prisoners. Aero planes over in early morning. more active all day. Went down to Bouilonville. Salvation Army-K.C. Red Cross and Y. M. C. A. Attended show and had cocoa and

walked back. 28th Div. now located there. German wordy
reply to Wilson
   Ruth's Birthday
   1st Engagement Anniversary

The Y. M. C. A. hut at Bouillonville

   23   Clear and Med. warm. Aero-planes very active
all day. Went down to Thiaucourt salvaging. U. S.: CAC-90
tied up to o.p. for our use. Went on shift at 17 oclock. Ger-
man Aero-planes did a whole lot of bombing. Ordered to be
ready to go ahead any time. Allied barrage dropped at 19:30
for 20 min.

An American CAC Gun

C.A.C. stood for Coast Artillery Corps. Prior to World War I, the U. S. Artillery was divided into two branches--the Field Artillery and the Coast Artillery. Members of the Field Artillery were nicknamed "Redlegs" after the red stripes on their pants legs. The troops of the Coast Artillery were known as "Cosmoliners." This name was derived from the preservative compound cosmoline that was greased on coast guns to protect them from the deteriorating effects of the sea. In France, the C.A.C. operated large caliber guns all over the front. The C.A.C. in effect became America's heavy artillery in World War I.(22)

24   _Fogg-Cloudy-Cool_ _Very quiet under the curtain of nature. Hun threw some gas over in afternoon. Hun reply given to Wilson. Sure mix up of words._

President Wilson's reply to the second German note forced Prince Maximilian of Baden to call an emergency War Cabinet on October 17. At this meeting, General Erich Ludendorff summarized the dilemma facing the German government with one simple question: Should it surrender unconditionally to the Entente or call on the German people to fight a last desparate battle for the Fatherland? Oddly enough, General Ludendorff who had only days before called for a cessation of hostilities now supported the latter alternative. Prince Max, however, was unmoved by his military commander's newfound courage. In the end, after a careful review of existing German military resources, the Chancellor concluded he could not ask the German people to commit to an effort that was unlikely to succeed. The German government sent a third message to President Wilson on October 20. The note, received by the U.S. on October 23, promised a cessation of unrestricted U-boat activity and a complete acceptance of all American requirements, both political and military, for an armistice:

In accepting the proposal for the evacuation of the occupied territories the German Government has started from the assumption that the procedure of this evacuation and of the conditions an armistice should be left to the judgement of the military advisers and that the actual standard of power on both sides in the field has to form the basis for arrangements safeguarding and guaranteeing this standard. The German Government suggests to the President to bring about opportunity for fixing the details. It trusts that the President of the United States will approve of no demand which would be irreconcilable with the honor of the German people and with opening a way to a peace of justice.

The German Government protests against the reproach of illegal and inhumane actions made against the German land and sea forces and thereby against the German people. For the covering of a retreat, destructions will always be necessary and are insofar permitted under international law. The German troops are under the strictest instructions to spare private property and to exercise for the population to the best of their ability. Where transgressions occur in spite of these instructions the guilty are being punished.

The German Government further denies that the German Navy in sinking ships has ever purposely destroyed lifeboats with their passengers. The German Government proposes with regard to all these charges that the facts be cleared up by neutral commissions. In order to avoid anything that might hamper the work of peace, the German Government has caused orders to be despatched to all submarine commanders precluding the torpedoing of passenger ships, without, however, for technical reasons, being able to guarantee that these orders will reach every single submarine at sea before its return.

As the fundamental conditions for peace, the President characterizes the destruction of every arbitrary power that can be separately, secretly and of its own single choice disturb the peace of the world. To this the German Government replies: Hitherto the representation of the people in the German Empire has not been endowed with an influence on the formation of the Government. The Constitution did not provide for a concurrence of the representation of the people in decisions on peace and war. These conditions have just now undergone a fundamental change. The new Government has been formed in complete accord with the wishes of the representation of the people, based on the equal, universal, secret, direct franchise. The leaders of the great parties of the Reichstag are members of this Government. In the future no government can take or continue in office without possessing the confidence of the majority of the Reichstag. The responsibility of the Chancellor of the Empire to the representation of the people is being legally developed and safeguarded. The first act of the new Government has been to lay before the Reichstag a bill to alter the Constitution of the Empire so that the consent of the representation of the people is required for decisions on war and peace. The permanence of the new system is, however, guaranteed not only by constitutional safeguards, but also by the unshakable determination of the German people, whose vast majority stands behind these reforms and demands their energetic continuance.

The question of the President, with whom he and the Governments associated against Germany are dealing, is therefore answered in a clear and unequivocal manner by the statement that the offer of peace and an armistice has come from a Government which, free from arbitrary and irresponsible influence, is supported by the approval of the overwhelming majority of the German people.(23)

25   *Fogg-Cool. Very quiet except for gas and H. E. barrage then Allies threw over around 3 Q. M.-Very noisy 30 min. C. A. C.-8" moved in the valley behind. Wilson handed Kaiser Bill his reply referred him to Gen Foche* [Foch] *but he will deall with German people.*

Went down to Burbon* [Bourbonne] *and took bath 2 months? I sure remember the Y. M. deal pulled off.

A U.S. C. A. C. 8 in Howitzer

The U. S. Coast Artillery Corps. mounted a number of high caliber coastal artillery pieces onto railway cars for use at

the front during World War I. Weighing well over 32,000 lbs.,
the 8 inch seacoast gun was capable of firing a 200 lb. projectile
nearly 12 miles.(24)

President Wilson swiftly replied to the third German note
incredibly again without Allied collaboration. Drafted on October 23, the communique continued the harsh rhetoric that had
been present in President Wilson's second note to the German
government. The message laid out to the Germans was clear--
force the abdication of Kaiser Wilhelm II or surrender unconditionally:

> Having received the solemn and explicit assurance of the
> German Government that it unreservedly accepts the terms of peace
> laid down in his address to the Congress of the United States on the
> 8th of January, 1918, and the principles of settlement enunciated in
> his subsequent addresses, particularly the address of the 27th of
> September, and that it desires to discuss the details of their
> application, and that this wish and purpose emanate, not from those
> who have hitherto dictated German policy and conducted the present
> war on Germany's behalf, but from Ministers who speak for the
> Majority of the Reichstag and for an overwhelming majority of the
> German people; and having received also the explicit promise of
> the present German government that the humane rules of civilized
> warfare will be observed both on land and sea by the German armed
> forces, the President of the United States feels that he cannot decline
> to take up with the Governments with which the Government of the
> United States is associated the question of an armistice.
>
> He deems it is his duty to say again, however, that the only
> armistice he would feel justified in submitting for consideration
> would be one which should leave the United States and the powers
> associated with her in position to enforce any arrangements that may
> be entered into to make a renewal of hostilities on the part of
> Germany impossible. The President has, therefore, transmitted his
> correspondence with the present German authorities to the
> Governments with which the Government of the United States is
> associated as a belligerent, with the suggestion that, if those
> Governments are disposed to effect peace upon the terms and
> principles indicated, their military advisers and the military advisers
> of the United States be asked to submit to the Governments

associated against Germany the necessary terms of such an armistice as willfully protect the interests of the peoples involved and ensure to the Associated Governments the unrestricted power to safeguard and enforce details of the peace to which the German Government has agreed, provided they deem such an armistice possible from the military point of view. Should such terms of armistice be suggested, their acceptance by Germany will afford the best concrete evidence of her unequivocal acceptance of the terms and principles of peace from which the whole action proceeds.

The President would deem himself lacking in candour did he not point out in the frankest possible terms the reason why extraordinary safeguards must be demanded. Significant and important as the constitutional changes seem to be which are spoken of by the German Foreign Secretary in his note of the 20th of October, it does not appear that the principle of a Government responsible to the German people has yet been fully worked out or that any guarantees either exist or are in contemplation that the alterations of principle and of practice now partially agreed upon will be permanent. Moreover, it does not appear that the heart of the present difficulty has been reached. It may be that future wars have been brought under the control of the German people, but the present war has not been; and it is with the present war that we are dealing. It is evident that the German people have no means of commanding the acquiescence of the military authorities of the Empire in the popular will; that the power of the King of Prussia to control the policy of the Empire is unimpaired; that the determining initiative still remains with those who have hitherto been the masters of Germany. Feeling that the whole peace of the world depends now on the plain speaking and straightforward action, the President deems it is his duty to say, without any attempt to soften what may seem harsh words, that the nations of the world do not and cannot trust the word of those who have hitherto been the masters of German policy, and to point out once more that in concluding peace and attempting to undo the infinite injuries and injustices of this war the Government of the United States cannot deal with any but veritable representatives of the German people who have been assured genuine constitutional standing as the real rulers of Germany. If it must deal with the military masters and monarchical autocrats of Germany now, or if it is likely to have to deal with them later in regard to the international obligations of the German Empire, it must demand, not peace negotiations, but surrender. Nothing can be gained by leaving this essential thing unsaid. (25)

The German High Command: Kaiser Wilhelm II, Field Marshall Paul Von Hindenburg, and General Eric Ludendorff

26   Rain and cool Very quiet except for a few Fritz put over Gas and H. E.

Went on post 17:00 oclock. Quiet night Read mail Oct 2nd from States

Notes

Oct 22--Germans sent wordy reply note to Wilson

Oct 25   Pres Wilson replied on note turning Germany down

a show down.

27 Sunday

Very quiet day during the day. Artilary 150's moved in the valley ahead. German opened 18:00 oclock a barrage. Allies countered the barrage and gave them hell for a couple of hours. Came off post at 16:30

28 Clear and cool Went to Central and got full winter equipment. Nothing in particular except Artilary moving in. Got my last months pay-62 Francs. Signed pay roll for Oct.

*28th   Clear and cool Very quiet. Nothing doing
except a little ranging of our artilary. 150's Howizers moved
in. 210's Moved out. Battery of 90's pulled out. Wiz--Bang.*

A U. S. 150mm Howitzer

The 150's mentioned by Private Pfennig were most likely
French-made Schneider 150mm Howitzers, the standard long-
range gun of both the French and American armies during World
War I. The artillery piece was a howitzer by design; it could fire
at a very high trajectory. The cannon could hurl a 95 lb. shell
well over seven miles. The Schneider 150mm Howitzer was later
manufactured in the United States. It became the standard me-
dium range howitzer for the U. S. Army until the 1940's. (26)

29th   Clear and cool day heavy frost.
Very quiet. Aero-planes very active not battles in the
air.   *Ac-Ac's open most of time. Went on duty at 17:10. Night
very quiet except for gas on front lines.*
Austria hand up Germany sent another note.
What the hell do they want.

"Ac-Ac" was standard military slang for antiaircraft fire.
With the successful introduction of aircraft as military weapons
in World War I, it became necessary for troops on the ground to
defend themselves from aerial attack. Initially, the U.S. Army

depended on 3 inch coastal artillery pieces fastened onto trucks to provide ground protection. Later in the war, 75mm cannons mounted on mobile trailors were used as antiaircraft weapons.(27)

When he received President Wilson's latest cable of October 23, Prince Maximilian went straight to Kaiser Wilhelm II with an ultimatum--force the resignation of General Erich Ludendorff or find a new Chancellor. On October 25, the leaders of the German High Command, General Erich Ludendorff and Field Marshall Paul Von Hindenburg, left their military headquarters at Spa and traveled to Berlin with the hope of stiffening the government's resolve in the face of President Wilson's latest communication. It would be General Ludendorff's last meeting with the Kaiser. Under tremendous domestic political pressure, Kaiser Wilhelm II forced and then accepted General Ludendorff's resignation. On October 27, both Germany and later Austria-Hungary announced formally that future negotiations regarding an armistice would be conducted by governments which were subject to the people and in control of the military:

> The German Government has taken cognizance of the reply of the President of the United States. The President knows the far-reaching changes which have taken place and are being carried out in the German constitutional structure. The peace negotiations are being conducted by a government of the people in whose hands rests, both actually and constitutionally, the authority to make decisions. The military powers are also subject to this authority. The German Government now awaits the proposals for an armistice, which is the first step toward a peace of justice, as described by the President in his pronouncements. (28)

30   *Clear and cool Boucoup* [many]*-artilary active, ranging and tiped our concrete mixer over. Blew the farm to hell. Boucoup Aeroplanes work on both sides. German notes droped over our lines. Same go-to-hell move in their 88's made it lively on hill right with H. E. Came off post at 16:30*

At this point in the war, German airplanes often dispersed propaganda leaflets behind Allied lines. The German high Command was desparately trying to keep its forces from totally disintegrating in the face of the Allied onslaught. The distribution of such propaganda was no doubt an attempt by the Germans to slow the advance of Allied forces towards German soil. The following facsimile of propaganda was dropped over the Metz Front by the Germans in October of 1918:

The German People Offers Peace

The new German government has this programme.
"The will of the people is highest law."
The German people wants quickly to end the slaughter.
The new German popular government therefore has offered an
ARMISTICE
and has declared itself ready for
PEACE
on the basis of justice and reconciliation of nations.

It is the will of the German people that it should live in peace with all peoples, honestly, and loyally.

What has the new German popular government done so far to put into practice the will of the people and to prove its good and upright intentions?

a)The new German government has appealed to President
   Wilson to bring about peace.

It has recognized and accepted all the principles which President Wilson proclaimed as a basis for a general lasting peace of justice among the nations.

b)The new German government has solemnly declared its
   readiness to evacuate Belgium and to restore it.

c)The new German government is ready to come to an honest
   understanding with France about,
                    Alsace-Lorraine

d)The new German government has restricted the **U-boat War**

No passenger steamers not carrying troops or war material will be attacked in future.

e)The new German government has declared that it will
   withdraw all German troops back over the German frontier.

f)--The new German government has asked the Allied
Governments to name commissioners to agree upon the
practical measures of the evacuation of Belgium and
France.

These are the deeds of the new German popular government.
Can these be called mere words, or bluff, or propaganda?

Who is to blame, if an armistice is not called now?

Who is to blame if daily thousands of brave soldiers needlessly
have to shed their blood and die?

Who is to blame, if the hitherto undestroyed towns and villages
of France and Belgium sink in ashes?

Who is to blame, if hundreds of thousands of unhappy women
and children are driven from their homes to hunger and freeze?

The German people offer its hand
for peace.(29)

*31   Clear and cool Salvation Army moved into
Thiaucourt. Went down to pay them a visit. Fritz new it and
dropped some 88's in every fifteen minutes beginning at
14:00 to 16:00 oclock.*

Got mail Oct. 4th

Austrian note made public in paper.

*Infantry went over the top with little barrage and
straightened out line brought in prisoners.*

Thiaucourt

On October 29, the Austro-Hungarian government sent the following cable through the Swedish Foreign Minister to President Wilson:

> In reply to the note of President Wilson to the Austro-Hungarian Govenment dated October 18[19] of this year, with regard to the decision of the President to take up with Austria-Hungary separately the question of armistice and peace, the Austro-Hungarian Government has the honor to declare that it adheres to both the previous declarations of the President and his opinion of the rights of the peoples of Austria-Hungary, notably those of the Czecho-Slovaks and the Jugo-Slavs, contained in his last note. Austria-Hungary having thereby accepted all the conditions which the President had put upon entering into negotiations on the subject of armistice and peace, nothing, in the opinion of the Austro-Hungarian Government, longer stands in the way of beginning those negotiations. The Austro-Hungarian Government therefore declares itself ready to enter, without waiting for the outcome of other negotiations, into negotiations for a peace between Austria-Hungary and the Entente states and for an immediate armistice on all the Austro-Hungarian fronts and begs President Wilson to take the necessary measures to that effect. (30)

Developments + Notes of Oct.

Allies made big gains.
Germany made all kinds of diplomatic offers.
Allies terms Unconditional surrender.
Austria on knees asks for separate Peace and terms.
Bulgaria Surrendered.
Turkey on last legs and surrendered.

Can the Kaiser!
    Tin the Teut!
Pickle the Prussian!
    Brine the Brute!

When the boys get home
    After fighting good and true
You'll know yes where your place is
    When they take a look at you

Bulgaria sought a cessation of hostilities on September
26. Turkey quit the war on October 30.

French General Ferdinand Foch and an unidentified American officer.

Bombardment at the front--Air action--Flash Ranging--
Rumors of armistice--Armistice signed--11-11-11--Jalny--
Howe Post roster--Notes on Stay in "Death Valley"--Army of
Occupation--Dudelange--Thanksgiving--"Thoughts"

NOVEMBER 1918

Nov. 1918

1   *Clear and cool heavy frost.*
    Little ranging during the day. 2nd + 7th Div.
moved in. 5th Div-Artilary. Avions all over. No battery only
Ac-Ac's and M.G. Nothing doing till 23:50 when Fritz threw
1000 gas shells into Bois de Fay.
    Went on shift at 17:00.
    Turkey give over the Darenenlls [Dardanelles]
Germany Surpriz the world in 24 hours.

The 2nd and the 7th were Regular Army Divisions that entered the sector to relieve elements of the 42nd and the 28th Divisions respectively. The 5th Field Artillery Brigade had been detached from the 5th Division for use by the 7th Division on October 10. The 5th Field Artillery Brigade consisted of the 19th, 20th, and 21st Field Artillery Regiments and the 5th Trench Mortar Battery. The 19th and 20th employed 75mm artillery pieces, and the 21st fired 155mm Howitzers.(1)

Avion is a French word meaning airplane. Ac-Ac and M.G. are abbreviations for antiaircraft and machine gun fire.

On October 30 Turkish delegates boarded the British warship *Agamemnon* at Port Mudros, Lemnos. There, they signed an armistice that among other things opened the Dardanelles and the Bosphorus and allowed Allied access to the Black Sea. By treaty, the Allies occupied all military installations in the area of the Dardanelles and the Bosphorus.(2)

2   *Clear-Rain and Cool.*
    At 4:30 Allies put over heavy barrage on left
Germans came over on the right but got gas and H.E. Active
till 10:00 oclock. Avions active. German balloons moved up.
Austria begs for rapid action. Italians have them going.
Germany give way approx 10 miles Verdun to Sea

3d   *Sunday Clear and warm.*
         Put on heavy underwear. Germans put over
light barrage about 4:30. Avions active. American planes
very active. Aside from this a quiet day. Went down to Salva-
tion Army Hut--had doughnuts. Received issue from Red
Cross. Boche use search lights to locate aeroplanes by angles.

Salvation Army doughnuts

The doughnuts provided by the Salvation Army were very
popular with the American troops. According to Salvation Army
lore, the women volunteers at the Montiers hut were the first to
come up with the idea of frying doughnuts for the soldiers:

   The Salvation Army lassies at Montiers were in
consultation. Their supplies were all gone, and the state of the roads
on account of rain was such that all transportation was held up. They
had been waiting, hoping against hope, that a new load of supplies
would arrive, but there seemed no immediate promise of that.
   "We ought to have something more than just chocolate to
sell to the soldiers, anyway," declared one lassie, who was a
wonderful cook, looking across the big tent to the drooping
shoulders and discouraged faces of the boys who were hovering
about the Victrola, trying to extract a little comfort from the records.
"We ought to be able to give them some real home cooking!"
   They all agreed to this, but the difficulties in the way were
great. Flour was obtainable only in small quantities. Now and then
they could get a sack of flour or a bag of sugar, but not often. Lard

was also a scarce article. Besides there were no stoves, and no equipment had as yet been issued for ovens. All about them were apple orchards and they might have baked some pies if there had been ovens, but at present that was out of the question. After a long discussion one of the girls suggested doughnuts, and even that had its difficulties, although it really was the only thing possible at the time. For one thing they had no rolling-pin and no cake-cutter in the outfit. Nevertheless, they bravely went to work. The little tent intended for such things had blown down, so the lassie had to stand out in the rain to prepare the dough.

The first doughnuts were patted out, until someone found an empty grape-juice bottle and used that for a rolling pin. As they had no cutter they used a knife, making them in shape like a cruller. They were cooked over a wood fire that had to be continually stuffed with fuel to keep the fat hot enough to fry. The pan they used was only large enough to cook seven at once, but that first day they made one hundred and fifty big fat sugary doughnuts, and when the luscious fragrance began to float out on the air and word went forth that they had real "honest-to-goodness" home doughnuts at the Salvation Army hut, the line formed away out into the road and stood patiently for hours in the rain waiting for a taste of the dainties. As there were eight hundred men in the outfit and only a hundred and fifty doughnuts that first day, naturally a good many were disappointed, but those who got them were appreciative. One boy as he took the first sugary bite exclaimed: "Gee! If this is war, let it continue!"

The next day the girls managed to make three hundred, but one of them was not satisified with a doughnut that had no hole in it, and while she worked she thought, until a bright idea came to her. The top of the baking-powder can! Of course! But how could they get the hole? There seemed nothing just right to cut it. Then, the very next morning the inside tube to the coffee percolator that somebody had brought along came loose, and the lassie stood in triumph with it in her hand, calling to them all to see what a wonderful hole it would make in a doughnut. And so the doughnut came into its own, hole and all.

That was at Montiers, home of the doughnut. . .

It wasn't long before the record for the doughnut makers had been brought up to five thousand a day, and some of the unresting workers developed "doughnut wrist" from sticking to the job too long at a time.(3)

> **4th   *Clear and warm.***
> ***Very quiet except for heavy barrage on left***
> ***from 4:30-8-00. Doughboys went over but could only find***
> ***three at a machine gun.***
> ***Austria signed Armistice at 14:30 and went into effect***
> ***at 15:00 oclock.***
> ***Walked over to Bouilonvile 46 Div in and 64 Div at***
> ***Thiaucourt. 5 Div. Artilary on Front-2nd Eng. 2-5-7 on***
> ***Front. Went on post at 17:00 oclock.***

Doughboy was the old U.S. Army term for infantry soldier. The 1943 edition of *Funk and Wagnalls New Standard Dictionary of the English Language* suggests that cavalry troops humorously labeled infantrymen "doughboys" because of the buttons found on the infantry uniform. The buttons resembled globs of dough.

On November 3, 1918, special representative Colonel Edward M. House, a longtime friend and confidant of President Woodrow Wilson, cabled Washington from Paris with news that the Austro-Hungarian government had officially signed an armistice ending their participation in the World War. This armistice, however, was not an agreement between equal foes but more a listing of directives from victor to vanquished. There would be no mistaking Austria-Hungary as anything else but a defeated nation. Terms called for an immediate cessation of hostilities by all land, air and sea forces and a total demobilization of all Austro-Hungarian forces to prewar, peacetime levels. The repatriation of Allied prisoners of war would commence at once without reciprocity. All territories which had been invaded by Austria-Hungary would be evacuated immediately. Departing Austro-Hungarian forces would not be allowed to carry back any heavy military material. All railroad and military equipment would be left on site to be confiscated by Allied forces. Most of the Austro-Hungarian navy would also be surrendered to the U.S. Finally, the treaty provided for the occupation of and the freedom of movement on all Austro-Hungarian territory by the Allied nations and the U.S.(4)

It is difficult to decipher which units Private Pfennig was referring to when he mentioned the 46th and 64th Divisions. There were no such divisions in the A.E.F. during World War I. Most likely, the units mentioned were actually the 56th and 64th Infantry Brigades of the 7th Division. Elements of the 2nd, 5th, and 7th Divisions were stationed in Private Pfennig's locale at this time.(5)

> *5th*   *Clear and Warm.*
> *Ideal day in France but plenty of mud.*
> *4:20 A.M. old boys opened up on left. Plenty of aeroplanes over the lines. Got quadrosection 45 kilometers back. In 30 min had a German 150-220 located for A.I.S Day very quiet except for fly circus burning air of our balloons. Allies put two German planes down. Was one of the most picturesque nights on the front. Off duty 16:00 oclock.*

Flash Ranging Section No. 2 had four outposts. The observer on duty at each outpost was provided a panoramic map giving the location and range of enemy artillery. Each observer at his respective outpost was responsible for one quadrant of enemy territory. In this case, Private Pfennig's "quadrosection" was an area 45 kilometers behind the enemy front line.(6)

According to *USAF Historical Study No. 133, U.S. Air Service Victory Credits, World War I*, three German airplanes were shot down over the Toul Sector on November 5, 1918. The two planes Private Pfennig noted in his diary were most likely brought down by pilots of the 135th Observation Squadron and the 141st Pursuit Squadron. The 135th flew two-seater De Haviland DH-4's. Two pilots, First Lieutentant Charles C. Fleet and Second Lieutenant Leland D. Schock, and two observers, Second Lieutenant Otto E. Benell and First Lieutenant George L.

Usher, each received victory credits for destroying one of the
German planes. Five fighter pilots from the 141st were awarded
victory credits for bringing down the other. They were Captain
Hobart A. H. Baker, First Lieutenant Loris V. Cady, First Lieutenant Richard D. Shelby, Second Lieutenant Paul R. Chappell,
and Second Lieutenant Bryan Hamlin.

The story behind the 141st Pursuit Squadron and Captain
Hobart H. Baker in particular is worth some digression. The
141st was composed of Princeton University men. The squadron
took as its emblem the very same mascot of Princeton fame, the
orange and black tiger. "Hobie" Baker at the time was perhaps
the most celebrated athlete in the history of Princeton University.
An extremely versatile competitor, Hobie Baker excelled in both
football and ice hockey. He was credited with three air victories
during World War I and stood to return to the U.S. a legitimate
hero. Unfortunately, Hobie Baker died tragically in an airplane
accident in France after the war. Today, the "Hobie Baker Award"
is annually given to the most accomplished collegiate hockey
player in the U.S. The award is considered to be the "Heisman
Trophy" of college hockey.(7)

> **_6th_**   _Clear and warm_
> _Ideal day in France. Not much doing except for_
> _Artilary action on Bois de Henta and Thiaucourt. Went to_
> _Salvation Army Hut._
> _12:00 Received from A.I.S. Allies transfered terms to_
> _Germany. Artilary spy picked on line._

On November 1, the Allied Supreme War Council commenced a series of meetings at Versailles designed to outline terms
for a German armistice. On November 4, each Allied head of
government approved the final draft of terms. The duty of con-
veying the terms to a German delegation was entrusted to Marshal Foch and British Admiral Sir Rosslyn Wemyss. Colonel
House cabled the final version of the Armistice to President on
November 4.(See Appendix)

7th   *Cloudy-cool*
          Very quiet during day. Little cannonading at
night. Went up to F.L. on left.
          A.I.S. reported 20 German diplomats on way to
France. Went on shift at 17:00 oclock.

In his memoirs, Marshal Foch chronicled the events leading up to the signing of the German armistice:

> It was the night of November 6th-7th, at half-past twelve,
> that I received the first wireless message from the German Supreme
> Command. It gave the names of the plenipotentaries designated by
> the Berlin Government and asked that I fix a place of meeting; it
> added:
>> . . .The German Government would be glad if, in
>> the interests of humanity, the arrival of the German
>> delegation before the Allied front might cause a provisional
>> suspension of hostilities.
>
> I replied at once in these simple words:
>> If the German plenipotentaries wish to meet
>> Marshal Foch to ask him for an armistice, they should present
>> themselves at the French outposts on the road Chimay-
>> Fourmies-La Capelle-Guise. Orders have been given to
>> receive and conduct them to the place selected for the
>> meeting.
>
>> On the morning of the 7th I was informed that the German
>> plenipotentiaries would leave Spa at noon and arrive before the French
>> lines between four and five o'clock in the afternoon. Measures were
>> taken, by both the French and German commanders, to stop the
>> firing on each side during the passage of the enemy delegation
>>> Accompanied by General Weygand, three officers of my
>> staff, and the British naval delegation headed by Admiral Wemyss,
>> First Sea Lord of the Admiralty, I left Senlis at five o'clock in the
>> afternoon and went by special train to the place chosen for meeting
>> the German plenipotentiaries--a spot in the Compiegne Forest, north
>> of and near the station Rethondes. My train was there run onto a
>> siding built for railroad artillery.
>>> The German delegation, having been constantly halted by

the blocked condition of the roads behind the German front, reached the French lines only at 9 P.M. and arrived at their destination twelve hours late. It was not until seven in the morning of November 8th that the train bringing them drew up near mine.(8)

> *8th*   *Clear + cool*
> *Very quiet except for avions for photos.*
> *Let open at 18:00 and we got it. One-two-three. 88's*
> *150's-210-340. A story all ther own. 30-88 duds on hell "were doing our duty keep on" Tunnel caught hell. Latrine full of holes. Thiaucourt got there share and gas.*
> *German plentipotentiaries crossed line around 2:00 oclock and handed terms at 11:00 with 72 hours*

> *Gen Von Gundel*
> *Herr Erzberger*   *S of Sate*
> *Count Oberndorf*   *Ambassador*
> *Gen Von Winterfield*
> *Capt. Vanselow*   *Navy*

A.I.S.-18:00 Kaiser + Royal Family Gone

The 340mm gun mentioned in this entry was more than likely a 380mm "Max" railway gun. This artillery piece consisted of a 380mm naval barrel mounted onto a railway car. Firing High Explosive shells weighing over 1,600 lbs., the cannon had a range of 29 miles.(9)

The German plenipotentiaries were Imperial Secretary of State Matthias Erzberger (president of the delegation); Imperial Envoy Extraordinary and Minister Plenipotentiary, Count Alfred Oberndorff; Major General Detlev von Winterfeldt, Royal Prussian Army; and Captain Vaneslow, Imperial Navy. General Erich von Gundell, Royal Infantry was relieved of his post as plenipotentiary.(10)

As late as November 9, Kaiser Wilhelm II had visions of quietly leading his army home to Germany. Events unfolding in Berlin, however, radically changed his plans. The leaders of the Social Democratic Party issued an ultimatum to Prince Max of Baden calling for the abdication of the Kaiser and the Crown Prince. If their wishes went unheeded, the Social Democrats predicted a mass exodus of their rank and file membership to the Independents and to the Bolshevik-inspired Sparticists. What would follow would undoubtedly be revolution in Germany. Initially, the Kaiser believed he could restore order in the Fatherland by leading his army back to Germany. After conferring with Field Marshal Von Hindenburg and a host of German Staff Officers at Spa on the 9th, though, the Kaiser was forced to face reality--the German Army was no longer his to command. For that matter, concerns were even raised with regards to the Kaiser's safety as the troops returned home.

As the Kaiser was contemplating his next move in Spa, Prince Max laid the groundwork for the inevitable. He announced the abdication of the Kaiser and the Crown Prince. With this news, the Sparticists boldly seized the Imperial Palace in Berlin, hung a red revolutionary banner from a balcony, and declared a soviet. At this moment, it appeared that the Sparticists were about to seize Berlin just as their Russian counterparts had seized Petrograd one year before. They might have were it not for the determined leadership of the head of the Social Democratic Party. Sensing the danger inherent in the situation, Philip Scheidemann rushed to the steps of the Reichstag and proclaimed a Socialist Republic. A new President of the German Republic was sworn in, and a crisis was averted.

Throughout this entire episode, Kaiser Wilhelm could only watch the telegraph. Now politically irrelevant, the Kaiser was urged by Hindenburg to seek asylum in Holland to avoid the possibility of being arrested and tried by the new government in Berlin. The Kaiser agreed and at seven o'clock Sunday morning, November 10, the imperial train carrying the royal family left the station at Spa bound for the Dutch frontier.(11)

9th   *Cloudy-rain-cool*
       Quiet a little artilary action. Allies movement of troops. German very active with Metz guns. Observations most impossible. Light barrage put over 19 prisoners taken on left very little resistance found. Had a story all its own. Amerx Avions went over for observations with violent artilary activity after. Germans hauling ass.
       A.I.S. Read at 22:40 oclock that Armistace with Germany had been signed.
       Lt. Wright made Capt. Wright C.O. of F.R.S. #2.

       Noted--B. T. Avery--CAC 15 died in France
       Shulten:-When the roll is called up yonder etc.

       A Saying.:-I think I see what I believe to be a piece of camaflage.

The quote above was made by Private William J. Schulten, Company D, Helena, Montana.

       Nov 10th   *Sunday*   *Cloudy-clear+cool*
       Allied artilary active from early morning. Fogg heavy raised later to find Germans and roads to rear crowded. Light barrage and over the top.
       5th + 3rd Infantry moved in. Guns moved up. Observation balloons brought up by post. Had chance to go in.
       Gen. Foche [Foch] *says sign the paper or drink the ink before 11:00 oclock on Monday.*
       Gen. Pershing says. "Metz in two days if left alone"
       A.I.S. at 22:40 reported Armistice Signed and the morrow at 11:00 hostilities cease. Was on phone as good news went throu.
       Went on post at 17:00
       Armistic Officially signed on 11th at 5:45

The 4th Corps Balloon Group and the 6th Corps Balloon Group were assigned to the Second Army at this time. The 4th consisted of the 15th, 16th, and 69th Balloon Companies. The 6th had only one unit, the 10th Balloon Company. At the close of the war, there were 17 balloon companies working on the American front.(12)

The first meeting between the Allied delegation and the German plenipotentiaries took place at 9 a.m. on November 9. At this session, German representatives complained vehemently at the harshness of the armistice terms. The gathering ended near noon. A German courier left the area at 1 p.m. with the text of the terms bound for the German General Headquarters at Spa. In the afternoon, individual conferences between the delegations were set up to satisfy the Germans' need for further explanation and clarification of the terms. The day ended without German acceptance.

On November 10, the two delegations exchanged papers relating to the conditions of the proposed armistice. At 6:30 p.m., General Foch sent a note to the German plenipotentiaries asking whether they had received acceptance by the German Chancellor. The Germans replied in the negative. Between 7 and 9 p.m., the German envoys received two cable transmissions from the German Supreme Command, the first signed by the German Chancellor and the second signed by Marshal Von Hidenburg. Both cables authorized the signing of the armistice. On November 11 at 2:05 a.m., the German delegation requested a meeting with their Allied counterparts. The session started at 2:15 a.m. Nearly three hours later, at 5 a.m., November 11, Marshal Foch, Admiral Wemyss, Secretary Erzberger, Count Oberndorff, Major General Wiinterfeldt, and Captain Vaneslow signed the Armistice.(13)

11th   Cloudy Heavy Fogg
Early morning very quiet. At 7:30 Germans opened up light barrage. At 8:30-Central called saying war would end at 11 bells and the Allied Artillary let loose. Made hell on

earth "Fire at will" till 11 bells when all was quiet. At sound bearing of X mins the bands started to play and the doughboys sing. The end after 4 yrs 2 mo 11 days
Was active duty at front 1 mo 15 days with F. R. S. and under shell fire. News reached news at 5:40 state time
_"11 - 11 - 11"_

"Calamity Jane," Battery E, Gun #2, 11th Field Artillery, 10:59.59, 11/11/18, Bois de la Haie

Sergeant Jesse R. Hinman, Company B, 29th Engineers, Astoria, Oregon recalled the last minutes of the war:

Within one hundred yards of our dugout in St. Benoit was a battery of 75s and the commander told us that at 9 o'clock they, as well as other artillery outfits in that sector, would be permitted to fire as many rounds as desired for a period of 15 minutes. The hour for celebrating the victory had arrived. I think every piece of American artillery participated in the bombardment. The solid earth shook to the roar of the guns. Between their thunder-like claps a new note began to weave itself into the uproar--the sharper clatter of rifle fire and machine guns. Others besides the artillery were celebrating. We dashed into the dugout and brought out rifles and automatics and, during the 15 minutes that followed, added our bit to the din.

The bombardment died away, but later orders were given that during the three minutes prior to 11 o'clock, as many rounds as possible would be fired.

With Parker, I stood in the doorway of the shack we used as a kitchen the last three minutes of the war. When the guns opened with the roar, which we had heard so many times during those eight months on the front, I looked at the French clock in the corner. It was 10:57. Was this truly the end? It was almost unbelievable that we were hearing the last barrage. The hands of the dial now point to one minute to eleven. There seems to be no abatement in the roar of the artillery. Another half minute slips past. There appears to be a slackening of the action, but the 75's back of our billets are as active as ever. A few seconds pass--they seem like minutes. Suddenly the firing ceases. There is silence--silence so great that it in itself is appalling. We look at the old French clock. We distinctly hear it tick off exactly six seconds--then it strikes the hour of 11.

The American artillery fire on the morning of November 11 was returned with equal spirit by the Germans, the enemy shelling the front line as well as the areas in the rear.

The sudden calm brought the "doughboys," in their fox holes, to realize that the wild rumor, of which they had been rather dubious, was the "right dope" after all. It took a few moments for the real meaning of the thing to dawn upon them. They laid down their rifles, and, jumping to their feet, sent three cheers re-echoing among the hills, where only a few minutes before could only be heard the roar of the cannon.(14)

The crew from Battery D, 105th Field Artillery, 79th Division, hoisting the flag

President Woodrow Wilson delivering news of the Armistice to a joint session of the U.S. Congress

12th Quiet on Front
All still in death valley-Went up to front line. Turned back by out post

13th Quiet on Front+cool
Went up to Jualny [Jalny]

14th Quiet on Front+cool
Went on post from 10 till 17 oclock. Dough boys still celebrating Some of 5th Div Artilary moved up.

[Editor's Note: The following is an extract of a letter from Clair M. Pfennig that was published in the *Bristol Press*. It can be found in the December 17, 1918 issue of the newspaper.]

Extracts from letters received from Clair M. Pfennig, in which the readers of the "Press" are interested.
Nov. 14, 1918
A Silent Front
Somewhere in France
All is fine and it sure does seem queer to be in the quiet once more and quiet it is. When I tell you I have heard noise I

really mean it. Yes, noise and then noise. The last day on the 11th at 8:30 o'clock one of those pretty barrages open up and by 9 it was in full operation both light and heavy in action. It kept up a tense tone and you could see the Khaki in groups already for the word "Go." It sure looked pretty from our grand stand seat. We had been waiting for the move. Being in direct touch with our base by wire we got the dope and at eleven bells like a pulling of one string, an everlasting jolt and silence prevailed. Just thirty minutes more to go and all was set for over the top and we were expecting to drive to Metz but Kaiser Bill hauled out and all came to a decided and quick end. Great rejoicing amongst the doughboys but it was hard to stop them as nothing but success was in front of them and the Hun was their aim. It ended without a doubt just as one of the greatest offensives was about to start. We had watched the peace moves day in and out and hoped if it was to end now it would before drive started as its loss of course would be great. Could be nothing else, and thirty minutes beat us to it. Thanks to the good Lord.

A talk which has started is how long before we will be pullin back. Our Corp is booked to go to Cologne but whether we will be is a question yet and we are still in our same billets awaiting orders. If they want us in Cologne there we will be. No matter to me, my duty is now to the finishing up of this task which we put the finishing touches on good and proper.

My grandfather's experience in the Civil War have nothing on mine and he could not have had any better luck than I have had. I got to the front proper to say the least. I do not know what was with me as luck. Don't need any lessons in dodging for I know how to hit the ground, slide for holes and make home runs if I never played football before. The nearest a 210 got to me was ten feet and that was plenty and then some to feel the jolt and get covered with dirt and lying there wondering if another was coming or to jump up and run. Those 210's or in fact the 150's as the pesky 88's

*bang are known as the "wizz bang." If you hear one hit you
know you are safe, same as in lightning, if you hear the crack
you are safe. On the nineth Fritz got excited and sure did put
some over for our amusement. Who he was trying to get as
agamble, at least I was at the lantern and I heard one coming
singing along slowly, then it started to speed up--a sign of
descent--followed by a bang. I asked no questions but made a
double quick slide for our dugout and next morning was time
enough to find out what part of the little house it hit. It
splintered up the side a little coming in one and out the other
(this was the fragment.) Well thanks to God that none of
them had Pfennig on them. I guess they had an extra (N) in
or out that time all right. These are a few experiences that I
bear in mind and some day I can tell you some war scenes
and sights we saw from our grand stand seat.*

General Pershing insisted on strict censorship throughout the war. The rules of censorship were enforced on journalists
and servicemen alike. Any hint regarding the location or movement of U. S. forces was eliminated from press dispatches and
personal correspondence. As a result of this practice, the typical
letter home from an American soldier carried only the line "Somewhere in France" to delineate the location of the writer.(15)

According to the regimental records of the state of New
York, both of Private Pfennig's grandfathers served in the Union
Army during the Civil War. Harvey J. Merchant, Private Pfennig's
maternal grandfather, was a member of the 90th New York Volunteer Infantry Regiment. Frank Pfennig, Private Pfennig's pa-
ternal grandfather, was mustered to the 45th New York Volunteer
Infantry Regiment. One can only speculate as to whose experiences Private Pfennig was alluding to in his letter home.

Born and raised in New York City, Harvey J. Merchant
was a clockmaker by trade. He stood five foot, five inches tall
and had grey eyes, a fair complexion, and light-colored hair. On
October 28, 1861, at the age of 25, Harvey Merchant enrolled in
the 90th New York Volunteer Infantry Regiment. He was muster-

ed in as a corporal and within a year was promoted to the rank of sergeant. After his reenlistment in 1864, Harvey Merchant quickly progressed up the ranks of the 90th New York. He became a first sergeant and then a sergeant major. For most of 1864, the 90th New York saw considerable action in the Shenandoah Valley. Alongside units of the Army of the Potomac and the Army of West Virginia, the 90th New York engaged in a bloody battle at Cedar Creek, Virginia on October 19. Later in the year, Harvey Merchant received a commission as a second lieutenant. He concluded his service career as a first lieutenant and commanded troops occupying the city of Savannah, Georgia. On February 9, 1866, Harvey Merchant was officially mustered out of the regiment and returned to private life.

Frank Pfennig was also a native of New York City. On November 1, 1861, he enlisted as a private in the 45th New York Infantry Regiment. Frank Pfennig was 28 at the time. The 45th New York was often referred to as a "High Dutch Regiment" because of the ethnic origins of its recruits. Following three years of service, Frank Pfennig reenlisted as a veteran in 1864. Although he remained a private throughout his entire military career, Frank Pfennig did participate in some of the most crucial battles of the Civil War. The 45th New York fought at both Chancellorsville, Virginia and Gettysburg, Pennslyvania. Nearly two-thirds of the 45th New York was either captured, wounded, or killed when the regiment was cornered in a back alley by Confederate sharpshooters within the city of Gettysburg. In the latter stages of the war, the 45th New York saw additional duty in Tennessee. Private Pfennig was discharged from service on June 30, 1865 in Nashville, Tennessee.(16)

15th   Quiet+very cool.
Ordered salvage wire ready to move with forth corp-
F R S #2 Second Army Lift went into central on faults move
Forth Corp + Second Army going

From September 17 through November 16 1918, the IV Army Corps occupied the Toul Sector and Thiaucourt Zone. It was composed of the following divisions: 1st, 2nd, 4th, 5th, 7th, 28th, 33rd, 35th, 37th, 42nd, 77th, 79th, 82nd, 88th (1st Brigade), 89th, 90th, 9nd, and the French 69th. On November 15, IV Corps was reconstituted from the 1st, 2nd, 3rd, and 4th Divisions and ordered to form part of the Third Army for the march into Germany.(17)

Howe Post
Sgt ftCl. Schinder

Pvt1stCl.	_William_	_Schulton_[Schulten]	_Helena Mont._
Corp.		_Armstrong_	_St. Paul Min._
		Wynkoop	
		Hoffmier [Hueffmeier]	
		Pfennig	
Pvt.1stCl.		_Bradshaw_	_Jackson Cal._
		Stone	_Mich_
		Neff	_Sunbury Pa._
		Burge [Berg]	
Corp.		_Tucker_ [Tuckner]	
		Benzen [Bentzen]	_N.Y._
		Wilcox	_Parish N. Y._
		Eaton	

Posts F. R. S. #2
Cotton Post--Rock Post--Howe Post--Chambers Post

_G. Z. C._
C.O. Capt Wright
    Liuet Lustcom [Luscombe]
    _"_   _Barrow_
    Master Eng. Brewster
    Sgt. Hinton-Central
    _"_   _Greisley_ [Graysle] _Lines._

Members of Howe Post, F. R. S. #2:

Sergeant First Class Feador Schinder, Co. D, Carney's Pt.,
New Jersey

Private First Class William Schulten, Co. D, Helena,
Montana

Corporal Ernest R. Armstrong, Company C, St. Paul,
Minnesota

Private Mark P. Wynkoop, Company C, Bismarck, North
Dakota

Private William F. Huefmeier, Company E, St. Paul,
Minnesota

Private Clair M. Pfennig, Company D, Bristol,
Connecticut

Private First Class Donald Bradshaw, Company C,
Amadar, California

Private Ransom Stone, Company C, Port Huron,
Michigan

Private Harold E. Neff, Company D, Sunburg,
Pennsylvania

Private Herbert B. Berg, Company C, Minneapolis,
Minnesota

Corporal John H. Tucknor, Company C, British
Columbia, Canada

Private Aage C. Bentzen, Company C, Troy, New York

Private Fred B. Wilcox, Company C, Parishville,
New York

Private Frank Eaton, Company C, Richmond, Indiana

General Zone Command

Commanding Officer Captain Jefferson D. Wright, Commerce,
Georgia

Second Lieutenant Carl B. Luscombe, Joplin, Missouri

Second Lieutenant George M. Barrow, Pittsburgh, Pennsylvania

Master Engineer Brewster

Sergeant Charles W. Hinton, Company C, Seattle, Washington

Sergeant Charles B. Graysle, Company C, Spencerville, Ohio

16th *Cool but clear*
Belgium-French American prisoners turned over at
Raubal [Roubaix]. Very quiet and seemed good.

Notes of Week

8 **Germans handed Armistice**
11 **Signed at 5:40**
War ended @11:00

Notes of Stay in Death Valley

14 horses and Artilary Out fit. Direct hit on three guns of
battery. One officer-four men- Humming Bird-14" Boy
Shrapnell-throu Latrine
46 Duds
Under fire at Thiaucourt Dud on track Direct hits on dug-
outs Flying Circus and balloon

The "Humming Bird" was a 14 inch, 50 caliber naval gun
mounted on a railway mount.(18)

17th *Sunday Cloudy-cool*
Quiet-not feeling to good. Took castor oil Army
Medicine. Gen Foche [Foch] lead Franco-American troop into
Metz. First of train occupying German territory.
Orders to leave on the morrow. All posts called in for
night.
Lieut Barrow note on censoring. Some joke. Traded
with prisoners.

———————·———————

Notes
Sept 18 202 Batteries located 800 guns.
to Nov 11th Some on Metz Forts.

Major to Private:-What out fit do you belong to"." F. R.S.
"replied. "Oh excuse me"

The Allied parade into Metz

American troops were ordered not to fraternize with German troops. Most U.S. soldiers ignored the command. Mingling between American and German troops commenced almost as soon as the guns ceased firing on November 11. A member of the 29th Engineers recalled the commingling of former adversaries on that day:

> But what is this--pouring from the enemy machine gun nests and entrenchments into No Man's Land was a streak of figures in green colored uniforms, their hands raised to show they bore no arms. Amazed the Americans waited. Then they noticed that the Germans were grinning and making every effort to show that they were friendly. Slowly the American "doughboys" made their way over to the spot where the visitors had halted. The enemy on whom they had been hurling shells and bullets only a few minutes before were grinning and extending their hands. The Americans were not so enthusiastic. Coldly a few "doughboys" shook the hand of a German, others disdainfully refused to fraternize.
>   . . . Then the Germans displayed an assortment of souvenirs. That settled the matter. The Americans produced tobacco, soup, leather vests, etc. For these the Germans traded lugers, wound badges, iron croses, rings, coins, and belt buckles, so dear to the heart of the "doughboy."(19)

Captain J. D. Wright drafted the following memorandum which officially summarized the experiences and the accomplishments of Flash Ranging Section No. 2 during its service on the front line:

Memorandum

December 7, 1918

Attached is completed list of different enemy batteries located by Flash Ranging Section No. 2 from September 3, 1918 to November 11, 1918, which was from time of taking over S.R. O. T. 62 (French) to the cessation of hostilities.

The total number of batteries was 202, of which 19 were located twice or more, and 13 of which were located a few meters different from previous locations.

About 40 per cent of the total number shown were verified by other sources of information.

During the period of operation we calibrated 4 guns of 240 calibre; 3 guns of 270 calibre and several guns of 155 calibre. All calibrations were a success, except one of 240 calibre and one of 155 calibre. Besides the calibrations, we were able to direct the fire of our own artillery on many targets.

One-half of the time was taken up with General Intelligence and German artillery activity, in which were were able to keep the Corps and Division A. I. S. well informed as to the activity of the enemy in front of us.

During the period of operations the section participated in the St. Mihiel drive and was able to get two posts and central operations about 60 hours after the beginning of the attack. We were delayed 24 hours on account of heavy traffic and bad roads. The distance moved was about 20 kilometers. Transportation used was two trucks.

Our casualties were: 1 killed in action; 3 gassed in action; 6 accidently hurt, 4 to hospital; 10 sick, 6 to hospital.

On a separate sheet is shown the complete history of the section as taken from our "Morning Reports."

J. D. Wright

Capt., Engrs., U. S. A., Comdg. Section F. R. S. No. 2 (20)

[Editor's Note: The following is an extract of a second letter from Clair M. Pfennig that was published in the *Bristol Press*. It can be found in the December 17, 1918 issue of the newspaper.]

Dated--Nov. 17th, 1918

Having just received some more mail again after getting straightened out from the relax of the "11-11-11" That was a glorious time for us all right and everything is fine. I suppose you people beat us to the news by indication at least; sure must have by time. It was on the night of the 10th at 10.40 o'clock (by armytime 22.40) that I was observing and had the ear pieces on when central wired that A. I. S. reported armistice for the morrow at 11 and the next morning at 5.40 it was officially signed. By jove that was a big time all around. Not as you might have expected but of activity. It was sure hell on earth for the poor Germans. It was on the front where I was observing that the second army started over the top around Hautmont and extended to the east. I happened to be lucky as I look at it--my time at the glass being 9 p.m. to 12 p.m. on the 10th (army time 21 to 24 o'clock) and from 9 a.m. to 12 m. on the 11th. Well now the next is we are about to move. You are without a doubt reading in the paper of this date that General Foch is leading the Franco-American troops into Lorraine to Metz and Straussburg and as this is our salient we are about to go and then maybe to the Rhine, as the Americans are going to Cologne. We wonder if it may be us, but maybe not. Anyway I am glad F R S No. 2 is included in the 4th Corp and I happen to be in it. It's funny they didn't let some of the boys from the rear come up instead of leaving it for those who did the trick to say they went into Germany and to the Rhine.

Well I just went to look at the weather. The stars were shining and the moon was high. An ideal night all right and good and brisk take it from me but I love the out-door life. You understand we do not live in tents. I do not say we never lived in a dug-out because at F R S No. 2 it was the most comfortable _for all concerned. We could laugh at the old boys as they came in loaded with gas and that would come but the gas curtains we had very little trouble with it except a little sneeze and tear gas now and then. One nice thing was Fritz built all these dugouts and they were mighty good ones take it from me. They hated the Franco-American shells as their effect was awful._

      We are ready to have a parade through Germany and I am glad I have this opportunity of going on as only sixty out of ninety in this section have been selected to go. The rest will go back to mobilization and do all kinds of drilling and detail work till we come back so it does not mean the states any sooner. I expect to hit the States before Easter Sunday.

      Am glad to day I feel like myself again. It is the first day since we left for the front which was Sept 27 that I have felt like myself and it sure does seem good. When the front was silent for the first time in the last 52 months we all felt dazed but now we are all glad that it is over with.

                          C. M. PFENNIG

         Co. D, 29th Engineers F R S No. 2
           American Exped Forces.
Officers in charge F. R. S. #2
      Capt. Wright
      Lt. Barrows-Luskume [Luscombe] _attached to Park Art. Div. Corp._
      42 Div--Rainbow:-65-66-67-68
P. C. 4th Corp Park Bat
      Lt. Col Prince
F. R. S. #2   -6 Trucks Train
              2 Fords
              1 Motor + SideCar

      The 42nd Division contained two infantry brigades, the 83rd and the 84th. The 83rd Infantry Brigade consisted of the 165th and 166th Infantry Regiments. The 84th Infantry Brigade

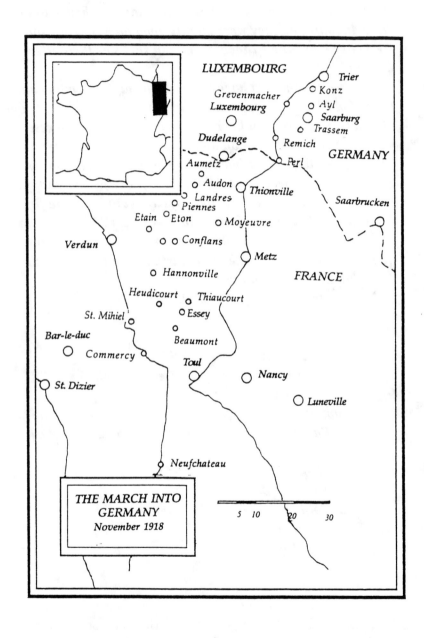

THE MARCH INTO
GERMANY
November 1918

was composed of the 167th and 168th Infantry Regiments.(21)

Notes of Trip F. R. S. #2

with

Army of Occupation

—————————·—————————

Army of Occupation

Div's ***1;2;3;4***		***Third***
32;42;		
4th Corp	***Army***	
F. R. S. #1 ***F. R. S. #2***		
Maj. Gen Muire U. S. A.		

From November 17, 1918 to May 11, 1919, the Third Army included the 1st, 2nd, 3rd, 4th, 32nd, and 42nd Divisions, the IV Corps, and Flash Ranging Sections #1 and #2. Nearly 230,000 men participated in the occupation. The Commander of the IV Army Corps was Major General Charles H. Muir.(22)

    18th   *Revealry - 3:00*
             Breakfast 4:00
             Off   *6:00 to join troop train*
Route Trip covered Envirsin - Pannes - Nonsard - Headicourt
[Heudicourt] - Hattonville - Billy - Hannonville -> St. Hilaire -
Moulotte - Allamont - Puxie Jeaudilizy - Buzy
             Passed front line at A. M.
             Put up for night A-1 at Buzy

    19th   *Clear and cool*
             Rested at Buzy Troops of train moved in. Inspection at
11:00 Accident not serious. Visited dam built to flood flats on

advance by Americans. Master Eng Brewster went back.

Sergeant George B. Howe, Co. D Portland, Oregon, provided a more detailed chronicle of the trip into Germany by Flash
and Range Section No. 2:

> It was with a glad heart that we left Eunezin loaded in six
> big trucks with our three officers and 29 men, to begin the first lap
> of our journey to Germany. Our first day's travel was very slow
> owing to the congested condition of the roads. It was a great
> pleasure for us to cross the famous Hidenburg line, the line that some
> of us had faced for nine months. The line that was supposed to be
> unconquerable, with its concrete pill boxes, deep dugouts and
> wonderful system of barbed wire entanglements. The line that all
> Germany has based its hopes on--and the line that was the goal of
> every soldier in France.
> The roads were filled with home-coming refugees, Russians,
> Poles and French. Many of whom had spent the last four years in the
> cruel prison camps and mines of Germany. Their bodies bore the
> marks of German kultur, but their hearts were clean and filled with
> new hope of the future, home and love ones. All stopped to watch
> the cheery, happy Americans as we passed by in our trucks.
> We passed village after village, not the little red-roofed
> villages that we had learned to love in France, but dirty, deserted
> villages and only a few hours before the homes of German soldiers,
> now desolate save for a lonely refugee or a barking dog, left to
> carry out the picture of desolation, which followed the footsteps of
> the retreating Huns. By night we had reached Buzy, another one of
> these deserted villages in Alsace-Loraine. Here we rested for five
> days--here we also had the misfortune to lose our First Sergeant,
> "Casey" Brewster, who accidently shot himself through the hand and
> was sent to the hospital.(23)

**20th   Clear and cool   Waited orders to move at Buzy
Swimming pool-dynamite in bridge, flood dams, boats
explosives on R-R**

**21st   Clear + cool   Waiting orders which came to
move on morrow at 8:00. Visited old Hindenburg Line. Dummy
Tanks. Shell holes all around it**

In the autumn of 1916, the Germans began construction of a series of strong rear fortifications along the Western Front from Cambrai to Metz. Each was named after a character from the epic German poem, _The Ring Saga_. The most famous of these fortifications was the _"Siegfried Stullung"_ or Siegfried Position. It covered the area between Cambrai and Quentin. Others included the _"Wotan Stullung,_ the _"Alberich Stullung,"_ and the _"Brunhild Stullung,"_ and the _"Kriemhilde Stullung."_ Each position was about ten miles in depth was made up of eight or nine belts of barbed wire that could be swept by well-placed machine-gunners. The Allies referred to this defensive network as the "Hindenburg Line."(24)

22_nd_ Clear + cool	
Revealry	**6:00**
Breakfast	**6:30**
Pulled Out	**8:15**

Route

    Buzy - Etain - Eton - Panloncourt - Bouligny - Mouriors- [Moveuvre] - **Piennes - Landres - Auton Le Roman** [Audun Le Roman] **- Bellidro - Luxemburg) - Aumetz - Abgrton - Dudelange**
Volmerange   12 000 population
    Shoot up
    Rail Road Centr:- Pioneer Div.
    Royal Parade followed by hill   A hard pull
-- -- -- Rested at Dudelange 3d City in size in Lux. Big Parade for coming. Put up in school house-gas-steam heat-running water
    German rear guard pulled out on 20th at 9: oclock - 11:00American advance guard came in by invitation of authorities. Some reception. Mines-Stores-Civilization spoke German for the first time since 1913
    Gen Pershing at Luxemburg.

Elements of the 16th Regiment, 1st Division crossing the Armistice Line at Etain, November 17, 1918

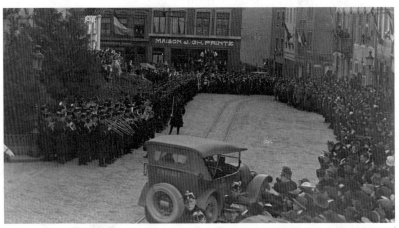

General Pershing arriving in Luxumburg with the Duchess of Luxemburg, November 21, 1918

The 32nd Division was nicknamed the "Pioneer Division." Its soldiers were Guardsmen from the states of Wisconsin and Minnesota. The division's shoulder insignia was the "red arrow."(25)

Sergeant George B. Howe continued his account of the trek into Germany with a vivid description of Luxembourg:

> The second lap of our "sight seeing" trip took us through Northern Lorraine and into Luxembourg. At Luxembourg--farewell deserted villages of Lorraine and No Man's Land--farewell your scenes of four year's strife--here is life and gaiety--fair daughters of the land in their quaint dresses were in every doorway and the streets, cheering us as we passed through their quaint little towns. That night at Indelange, one of the principal cities of the little principality, billeting in a steam-heated school house. The delighted populace fairly thronged up the hill to the school house to view the American soldiers, who accepted, without a blush, their praise and admiration of the children, who clung to us like barnacles. Hospitality was everywhere.
>
> Good people, glad of the opportunity to show their appreciation to be liberated from the Hun, took us into their homes, shared their meals and even their fine old French wine with us. The wine taken from the deepest recesses of their cellars, cunningly hid from the Germans. And for a few hours it flowed like water.(26)

23d *Clear + cool Formation at 10:00 A.M. Big Parade by 4th Corp. at 12:15. Houses wide open all around*
Americans f_ _ _ every thing they get. "Beaucoup Francs."
Meet Amer. woman in states till 20 20 years:-Lux. Army 250-4 M. G.

Prices at ease

$5 - 10 lbs Coffee		*$2.50 Eggs*
$4	*lb. Butter*	
Shoes	*200 mks* [Marks]	*Soxs Silk 30 mks*
Silk Tie	*8 "*	

Bread allowed 280 gr of bread-at start saw dust-sickness Now 250 gr of bread
Stars + Stripes made out of sheets 40 mks.

Wafels-   *1 mk.*   *pie i mk*
Ginger Bread 1 "
Apple Pie   8 "   *4 mks*
Coffee   1 "
Iron Mine + foundry
    80-90% Ore
    12 mks-wages
    Clothes 600 mks Bell "said" 55 Fks" Brownie
said "one button"

24th   Sunday Clear + cool Formation at 10:- Big
time and saw city.

25th   Cloudy-Rain-Cool
Note
    Germans "Look out for the Amer Dogs"
        "   gave people two days to evacuate
Dudelange-
Terms
    Remarks on 1st-26 Div. Posted

Luxembourg girls greeting their liberators

        26th   *Cloudy-Cool*

Routine

7:30	*First Call*
8:00	*Hot Cakes*
9:15	*Drill*
10:30	*N C School*
	[Non-Commissioned Officer School]
11:15	*F. R. Discussion*
3:30	*Dinner*
9:00	*All in*

Censorship lifted
Spanish Port Wine   ?

Stone - Bradshaw - Benson [Bentzen] *- Myself*

    27   Rain + cool-damp Felt like night before
Short Arm Inspection Dull day Village up line shot up.

    28   Rain-cool Was sure an exciting Thanksgiving-
Cafe de Commece [Cafe de Commissaire] *All night show and*
some time Stew-bread-butter-coffee On guard 4:00-6:00
Prices going up How did the gauge come in

According to Sergeant George B. Howe, Thanksgiving in Luxembourg was indeed a special event:

> Nothing was too good for the "American soldot." And then came Thanksgiving, the day that every good American celebrates with feasting. Some of us had spent our last Thanksgiving on the high seas, bound for Berlin, and here we were a year later, a little closer to the German capital, still hungry for a Thanksgiving dinner, with its Turkey pies--enough, enough and "canned Willie" staring us in the face--but the good people of Indelange, hearing it was a "grand fete" day in America, came to the rescue, and many lucky Flash Rangers had his knees under a clean tablecloth while a buxom Luxembourg mother bade him eat his fill of pie--yes pie, and apple at that--and other things that go to make Thanksgiving dinner a success.

To be sure, there was no turkey, as the Germans had taken them long ago, and right here it is well to say that if the American "doughboy" had known there was a pie waiting for him on the Moselle, that old Hindenburg line would have been broken long before it was shattered.(27)

29   *Clear-Cloudy-cool*
        On guard 10-12:00
        Took Bath 12:30 Luxembourg capital
Artilary Park detachment of 4th Corp some joke-

Howe-
Shilling There Capt. was with bells on.

        30th
                Clear Cool
                Inspection   *9:30*
                Mail   *3:00*

---   ---

Doit Sergent [Debit Sergeant]
        Has more to be pitied than censored
        More to be loved than dispized

--Thoughts--

        The proud heart may be in
want + yet cover up its needs with
showy pomp.

_____._____

        The good heart gives the
fragrent bloom to life; mans joyfullness
makes him live ripe old age

_____._____

*Most men can flatter you to
your face; those men seldom praise
you to your back*

———————.———————

*Hope is a common good;
it lingers when everything
else is gone*

Moselle River Valley--Toul--Joanne Arc Barracks--Officers of the 29th Engineers--Summary of Dates--Promotion--"French Pullman" to Donges--The 92nd Division--St. Nazaire-- MonToir--Christmas--U.S. Base Hospital #216

DECEMBER 1918

Dec. 1918

1   *Sunday Clear + cold Beau coup Girls*

2   *Revealry*   *5:30*
          Breakfast   *6:00*
          Pulled out   *7:10*
Route
          Dudelange
          Remmich [Remich]   *Grevenmacher*
          Conz [Konz]   *Trier (Treves) 6:30*

Hit the Mosel [Moselle] *River-Dec 1st at 3:00 3rd Div crossed*
          1st Div Crossed Dec 1st at 4:00
          FRS #2 reached bridge at 2:10
Waited orders + crossed at 2:30 Aeroplane dropped message while waiting delivered to us at Conz [Konz]. Order to return.
          Mosel [Moselle] *Valley at 12:30*
          Hills - vinardes - fields - walls - fords - Power line - Rail Road etc

3   *Trier (Treves) Lay over for - Rest*

4th   *Revealry at*   *5:30*
          Breakfast   *6:00*
          Pulled-out   *7:00*
Route
          Treves Conz [Konz] *Ayle* [Ayl] *Suarburg* [Saarburg]
Trassem (Hill) Menuck Kirf 1/2 Perl Apoch Thionville (Dudenhofer) some city 1/2 Truck detached;
          Took trolly side - Return got wrong car had to walk.
Some time 400 British Prisons in G--returning
          Big foundries; Aeroplanes etc.

U. S. troops on guard on the Moselle River

What is a colision

Joe	*Where two things come together*
Jack	*Had one down to my house last night*
Joe	*You did. What?*
Jack	*Had "Twins" Two things come together*

[Editor's Note: At this point, two pages were cut out of the diary.]

     5th

          Thionville

Revealry	*5:30*
Breakfast	*6:00*
Pulled Out	*7:20*

Route

Thionville   Metz
Pont a Mousson   Toul
Motes filled with water Firmbuildings walls etc
Trenches-concrete-city shot up. Was front line
Reached Toul at 2:30 Put up at "Joanne Arc
       Barracks" 2nd Bat. 29th Eng Assembling
Capt. Wright said follow me.

Sergeant George B. Howe closed his narrative describing the trip into German with the following entry:

> . . .orders came to move up into Germany. Of course, we wanted to see Germany, but how we did hate to leave Luxembourg, with its fine old people and rare old wine. We followed up the beautiful Moselle River to the little railroad center of Comz, Germany. Here we stayed for two days, and, much to our amazement of the populace, we destroyed nothing. Germany failed to make a hit with the boys, due, I think, to the fact that she was short on food, potato soup being their principal food, with black bread on the side. And then the people themselves regarded us more as intruders than the guardians of democracy, as though they expected us to ransack their houses and stores.
>
> Soon we received our orders to return to Toul, France, as our battalion was being reorganized there, preparatory for departing for America. It was great news. Of course, many of the boys wanted to proceed into Germany and see Coblenz, but the majority had seen enough of Europe and were anxious to see the old Statue of Liberty, and the rustle and bustle of a real American city.
>
> The return trip took us two days. The first night we stayed in Thionville, where the Germans had a large aviation camp. Here, also, were many returning English prisoners, and the "Tommies" had many interesting stories to tell of their experiences at Coblenz, Cologne and Frankfurt, in the prison camps and on the farms there.
>
> The next day we passed through the historical city of Metz, the stronghold of Lorraine, now occupied by French forces; the city that was the objective of the American Army so long--the city we would have surrounded and taken had the war continued. By night we reached Toul, France, and joined our various companies and F. R. S. No. 2 was no more.(1)

6th

> _Breakfast   7:20_
> _Assembled   10:20_
> _Straightened out checked up. F. R. S. #2_
> _Deassembled Reported to respective Co.-4:00_

7th

> _Reported to Co. D. 29th Engs._

———————— · ————————

Time   *F. R. S.*   *#3*   *10 days*
                  #2   *60*   "

Front   *Sept. 27 to 17th of Nov (FRS #3 27 Spt - Oct 7th)*
        Army of Occ.-to Dec. 7th

Those   **Offices**   **who**

Commanded   **&**   **Made**

F. R. S.   **+**   **S. R. S:**   **29th Eng.**

Col. Alexander - Pershing Staff Dean of Penn. Univ.

Major Lyman - C. O. FRS+SR.S Prof Science - Princeton

       Trowbridge state work C. O. - F. R. S. #1 Prof
                Princeton

Capt Bazoni Study in Eng. - Smith. Inst. FRS #1+SRS #1 -
                Special work in sound

Capt Ross .. worked with British + French Flash #1 U. S. A.
                C. O.

Capt Wright worked with British + French C. O. of FRS #1
                FRS #2
Chatau Therry [Chateau-Thierry] *to Metz*

     The officers cited in this entry were the "Founding Fathers" of the Flash and Sound Ranging Service for the AEF. In the summer of 1917, General Pershing arrived in France and established his General Headquarters at Chaumont. Colonel Roger G. Alexander (then Major) served on Pershing's General Staff as commander of the Topographical Division. This Corps of

Engineers unit operated within the Intelligence Section of Pershing's staff and was responsible for map-making, surveying, and ranging. General Pershing commissioned Colonel Alexander to head up an investigation of French and British flash and sound ranging methods.

General Pershing was very impressed with the effectiveness of Allied flash and sound ranging. In June of 1917, he cabled the War Department in search of physicists who could handle the technical aspects of ranging. Major Theodore Lyman (then Captain) and Colonel Augustus Trowbridge (then Major), both formally of the Signal Corps, were transferred to the Corps of Engineers, sent over to France, and charged with the task of developing a flash and sound ranging capability for the A.E.F.

Captain Charles B. Bazzoni (then First Lieutenant) had been an American civilian doing atomic research in London when the U. S. entered the World War. He volunteered his services to General Pershing's staff, was commissioned, and was sent to assist Colonel Alexander in selecting a suitable flash and sound ranging system for the A.E.F. Captain Bazzoni spent considerable time on both British and French fronts. He was assisted by Captains Blair A. Ross and Jefferson D. Wright (then both Lieutenants). Captain Bazzoni's final report to the General Staff recommended that the A.E.F. use the British "Bull-Tucker" system. Captain Bazzoni and Major Lyman later opened the first American Flash and Sound Ranging School at Fort de St. Menge, near Langres, in January of 1918.(2)

Camp in S. O. S.

A. P. O 784
Toul

Joan de - Arc Bks.

Co. D. 29th Engs.   **74th Engs.**

The various flash and sound sections of the 29th Engineers began to reassemble on November 22 at the Jeanne d'Arc Barracks, two miles outside Toul. Because of their movement into Germany, Flash and Ranging Sections Nos. 1 and 2 did not arrive until the first week of December. For the trip back to the U. S., the 29th Engineers was dissolved and reformed into the 74th Engineers.(3)

	1918			
Toul	*Dec. 7*	*to*	*Dec. 19*	
Donges	*Dec. 19*	*to*	*"*	*27*
Pont. Nantes	*" 27*	*to*		
Rousseau		*to*	*"*	*30*
	1919			
B. H. 216	*" 31*		*to*	*Feb 17*
St. Nazaire	*Feb 17*	*to*	*"*	*25*
Camp #1				
Atlantic	*25*	*to*	*Mar*	*11th*

U. S. A.

Dec. 7
> *Revealry   7:00*
> *Breakfast   7:15*
> *Inspection   9:00*
> *Duty   Bayonet*
> *Ordered to be ready to move*

8 Sunday Quiet Day-Cool Clear
Visited Nancy Toul   Given over sea equipment

9   Rain-Cool-Mud

10   Rain-Cool-Mud

11   Rain-Cool-Mud
Co. D 29th Engs to Co. D 74th Engs.
Made 1st Cl Private-36.60
2nd Bat. 29th Engs. to 1st Bat 74th Engs.

12   Cool-Rain-Mud

Generals Ferdinand Foch and John Pershing

13   Cool-Clear-Mud
President Wilson landed in France

On November 19, President Woodrow Wilson made the decision to personally attend the opening sessions of the Peace Conference to be held at Versailles. He arrived in Brest aboard the *U. S. S. George Washington* on December 13. One day later, President Wilson joined French President Jules Henri Poincare for a triumphal parade through the streets of Paris. Thousands cheered as the motorcade proceeded along the *Champs Elysees* and through the *Arc de Triomphe*.(4)

14th   Cool-Clear-Mud

You should treat your
Rifle as you would
your wife ----
Rub it all over
every night with
an oily rag.

15   *Sunday*   *Warm-Clear-Mud*

16   *Warm-Rain Mud*

17   *Cool-Rain-Mud*

18   *Cool-Rain-Mud*

19   *Cool-Rain-Mud*
Orders to prepare to move on morrow

Moved from Toul
to Donges

Deffanition - TNT - by member 92 Div.
        T. N. T.   Travel negroe travel.
Report from German O. P.
Situation.----
        26 Div holding front line
        92 Div relieved at night
        Germans put over strong gas attack:
Report ----
        Gas no use on those Americans officer. All they do is
turn black and fight on.

_____ .

Black troops of the 92nd Division advancing

When President Woodrow Wilson promised to make the world "safe for democracy," his words stirred the emotions of all Americans, white and black. Leaders in the black community quickly pledged their support for the war effort. Harlem minister Adam Clayton Powell, National Association for the Advancement of Colored People editor W. E. B. DuBois, and Tuskegee Institute president Robert R. Moton all encouraged black Americans to rally around President Wilson. These and other influential black spokesmen predicted that the World War would be a watershed event in black American history. Such hope was based on the premise that black men freely fighting and dying for their country would force the white majority in the U. S. to finally bestow on blacks all of the rights, privileges, and recognition of American citizenship which heretofore had been denied. When the U. S. Army unveiled plans to draft black as well as white men, the black community cheered with anticipation.

On October 24, 1917, the War Department created the 92nd Division, National Army. Its ranks were filled by black draftees. The troops in this division saw themselves as modern day "buffalo soldiers" and therefore used the buffalo symbol on divisional insignia. (Black men served in the U. S. Cavalry throughout the American West in the 1880's. Members of the Commanche tribe gave these troops the nickname "buffalo soldiers," after noticing a resemblance between the coarse fur of the buffalo and the hair of the black soldiers.) The command structure of the 92nd Division was somewhat unique for its time. While the division's staff officers were white, the 92nd's line officers were all black. This caused quite a bit of uneasiness among the whites in the Army who believed that black officers were naturally inferior. For that matter, the entire division endured much prejudice during its training near Des Moines, Iowa.

Under the command of General Charles Ballou, the 92nd Division landed in France in June of 1918. The discrimination the unit had experienced in the U. S. during training persisted overseas. Off-base freedom was restricted, mess facilities were segregated, and above all, contact with French women was prohibited.

Initially, most high ranking officers including General Pershing viewed the fighting capacity of the 92nd as incompetent. While this assessment was probably correct, white officers arrived at this conclusion in different ways. Naturally, bigoted whites blamed inherent ineptitude of the black race for the division's deficiencies. General Pershing, on the other hand, blamed superficial training for the 92nd's poor state of readiness. The lack of intensive, specialized training continued to plague the division in Europe. Throughout the first few weeks in France, elements of the 92nd were used as common laborers for the S. O. S. (Service of Supply).

The 92nd Division first saw action on August 23 in the St. Die Sector. Here, the division relieved French units along the front. No major engagements occurred. Simple patrol assignments were the rule. In late September, the 92nd was sent into the Argonne. The role of the 92nd in this offensive was far more complicated and perhaps beyond its competence at that point. Its performance was substandard at best. The 368th Infantry Regiment received the most criticism. Its men allegedly broke under shellfire and were relieved five days into the battle. The 368th's failure brought shame upon the entire division. As a result, the whole 92nd was ordered out of the Argonne on

October 5. In retrospect, the criticism leveled upon the 92nd was probably more severe because it was a colored division. Untested white units had broken under fire before and received much less scorn. Nonetheless, the 92nd's poor reputation relegated the division to patrol work for much of October.

The 92nd Division was given a reprieve of sorts later in November. It was assigned an advanced position in the push towards the German stronghold of Metz. Private Pfennig's diary entry undoubtedly refers to this assault. On the evening of November 10, the division's 365th, 366th, and 367th Infantry Regiments fought through heavy barbed wire to attack German positions. Under intense artillery fire, the black troops pushed forward through the night. In the course of the battle, the 92nd saved the French 56th Infantry which had been pinned down by hostile fire. This action alone would later win the division a _croix de guerre_ citation from the French.

The ironic timing of this attack was noted very specifically by Air Service Chief Colonel William (Billy) Mitchell in his memoirs. On the eve of the operation, Colonel Mitchell was in Toul and noticed that the Staff of the Second Army was preparing an attack for the next day. Personally, Colonel Mitchell thought the exercise foolish. Victory here, at this time, would give no great advantage to American forces. Casualties would most certainly be very high because of German resistance. Adding to Mitchell's feeling of dread was the fact that the division chosen to spearhead the attack was the inexperienced 92nd.

Colonel Mitchell's concerns were right on the mark. Results were disastrous, and given the fact that the war ended within hours of the assault, the entire episode appears tragic in retrospect. While each regiment reached its particular objective, the cost to the division was 500 casualties. This elevated the 92nd Division's total casualty number to 1,700, approximately 1.5 per cent of all U. S. casualties. The tenacity of the 92nd Division in its last fight though tempered some of the criticism that had plagued the unit earlier on. Even General Pershing openly praised the division's artillery units for their performance in battle.

In the Army's final analysis of the performance of the 92nd Division during World War I, it was noted that the unit suffered from poor leadership and training. Incompetent officers, both white and black, were blamed for the division's less than stellar performance. Once it had been seasoned under fire, the division performed at the level of many other white divisions. This seems to be proven out by the fact that 21 members of the 92nd Division won Distinguished Service Citations during the war. That total surpassed marks achieved by four other white divisions, the 35th, the 6th, the 81st, and the 86th.(4)

Dec. 1918

"Homeward Bound"

20 Friday

Revealry	*6:00*
Breakfast	*6:30*
Left	*8:30*

Went aboard train at 11:00
Got Stove for Fr. Pullman.

40 Homines
{8 Chevaux

Left Toul at   *4:00 P, M.*
Route:-

Mandres
Chateu Thierry [Chateau-Thierry]
Moselsect [?]
Commercy

Mandres
Commercy
Barleduc [Bar-leDuc]
Epernay

21 Sat   *430*

Route:-	*Manlesect*	*6 A. M.*
	LeMans	*11:30 P. M.-MP*

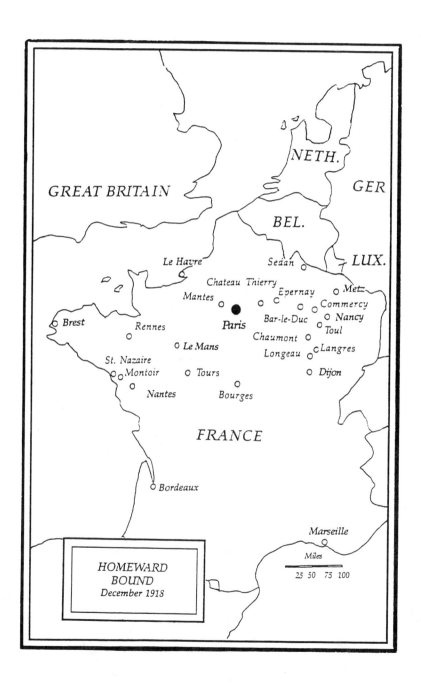

HOMEWARD
BOUND
December 1918

22 Sunday

 Pulled on side lines to St. Nazaire. Reached St. N at 1:20 P.M. Toul to St. N. - 45 <u>hr. 20 min.</u>

Red Cross served chocolate, cocoa bread and jam. Cigarettes etc. Switch and hell of time. Switched and at 5:30 P. M. got off; got on; got off--- Marched 1 1/2 kilo's Auto's to camp 6 kilo's at Donges. On river in swamp. U. S. making France-useful. Montoir big camp and wear houses

 <u>*Route:*</u>

 Montoir was the port depot of St. Nazaire, France. At the time, the facility was probably the largest ever constructed. Covering about 2,000 acres, Montoir provided over 4,000,000 square feet of storehouses and 10,000,000 square feet of open storage space. Montoir's wharf, located on the Loire River, could accomodate eight vessels.(5)

 23 Cool-rain-mud
  Truck detail to Montoir-Camp No 9.

 24 Cool-Rain-Mud-Clear
Orders to move 27th to Nantes for training under S. O. S. A thing to be remembered. A. O. A. must drill for S. O. S. before oversea Donges; dredging filling building

Note:-Geo Wash-22 days out: Capt German Spy (Fact.)

25

19

Christmas

1 in 8

Donges

A general view of the camp at Montoir

Received from Red Cross-YM
       3 Bars of Chocolate
       4 Pgs Gum
       5 Boxes Mallomars
Capt. Wright: 2lbs Chocolate
Dinner Tra Bon [Tres Bon]
       Menu Veal-Sweet Potatoe
              White Potatoes-Dressing
              Salad-Apple Pie
              Coffee

26   Clear-Rain-Mud   Lt. Kemper S. O. B. took us from camp for march. Flats of N. Jersey U. S. A. parallels Donges.

Second Lieutenant Darwin R. Kemper, St. Louis, Missouri

    27   Rain-Clear-Rain
          Revealry   6:00 A. M.
          Fall in   8:00
          Train   9:00
          Pulled out   10:00
              U. S. A. Engine

Pulled to Montoir switched to main lines for Nantes

Nantes P. O.	*1:30 P. M.*
Nantes Etet.	*2:30*
Started for Billets	*3:00*

Fell out at bridge.   Some
Damsells at Cafe - Sgt Robberts. [Roberts]

Billeted at Pont. Rousseau
Dance Hall-Beaucoup Madmozels Live town. Every-thing green. Prices for Americans

Harvey W. Roberts, Co. D, Utica, New York

28   Rain-Mud-Clear   Co. Routine

29   Clear-Mud   Moved Quarters to Old Mill-3 Kilo-East 64 up in atic.

30   Rain-Clear-Mud   Answered Sick Call

Experiences in U. S. Base
Hosp.
31   Rain-Clear   Reported Sick Call Temp. 104.8 Sent to U. S. Base Hospital #216-W-17
Wilcox - Hauleston [Houliston] *also Sin Clair* [Sinclair]*-Sgt. Colt-Shorty-also found ward-17 to Nantes from 74th Engs.*

Sheets and bed
3 Nurses in Charge
Salts + Asperin

Members of the 29th Engineers:
Fred B. Wilcox, Co. C, Parishville, New York
George M Houliston, Co. C, East Aurora, New York
Earl T. Sinclair, Co. C, Stillwater, Minnesota
Howard F. Colt, Co. D, New York, New York

JANUARY 1919

Jan 1919

Experiences Cont.
in
U.S. Base Hospital
France

Base Hos, 216 Grand Blottereau
A. P. O. 767 Nantes

Base Hospital No. 216 was created on November 1, 1918 at the Nantes hospital center. The unit was situated in a standard type A, 1,000-bed hospital of cement-fiber construction. In addition to its normal treatment assignment, the Base Hospital No. 216 was designated as a special hospital for all communicable diseases and all complicated cases of venereal disease. The facility became an evacuation hospital in January, 1919. Every patient evacuated directly to the U. S. was sent through this unit. Base Hospital No. 216 was demobilized on June 21, 1919.(1)

Doctors Ward 17
Capt. Wright   Luiet. Joy   Capt. Currie

Hospital-Chiefs   *Capt. Pratt*   *Capt. Kleinfelt* [Kleinpell]

Medical Personnel of Base Hospital No. 216
Lieutenant Colonel Robert B. Pratt, M. C.,
    Commanding Officer
Major Henry H. Kleinpell, M. C., Chief of Medical
    Service

Jan. 1919

    1   *Rain-Cool Temp. 3 times at night 3 times at
day Still running Sheets and spring bed*
        Pajamas
          Blue Pants
    {   *Pink Coat*
*Got Bath-1st since when. Nurse Miss McCloud. Battleship
and Duck*
        Base Hosp. 216 A. P. O. 767
        24-74th Eng. in 216

Notes

    *Hosp. Bldg.-30x150 50 Beds to Bldg. Made out of
two wall cement board. Cement floor and tar paper roof. 2
Stoves-soft coal. 1 Nurse to ward; 1 Ward Master; 2 Order-
lies*

    2   *Rain-Cool Temp. Steadied Sleep + take pills
Salts Took on usual sleep   Capt. Wright Capt. Currie*

    3   *Rain-Cool Temp. steadied Flo turned to
Brown Kittens as Miss Willeby called it*

    4   *Rain-Cool Started to feel better Temp 101.<u>0</u>*

    5   *Sunday Rain-Cool Temp going New Nurse.
Little crazy head. Alcohol bath.*

**6   *Rain-Cool Weather conditions cause condi-
tions. B. H. 216-B. H. 11 all in Park. Location known as Big
Swamp. 1916 under water four foot on wall. Dikes hold
river out***

*Night Nurse gave me alcohol bath. Starting of my
feeling better. chills ceased*

**7   *Rain-Cool Started to feel at home. Put from
liquids to light Diet. Pretty good.***

8   *Rain-Cool Futcher died*

Arthur J. Futcher, Co. D, Philadelphia, Pennsylvania

**9   *Rain-Cool Eats pas bon. Corn* [undecipher-
able word]*-Gold Fish Peas-Corn etc***

10   *Rain-Cool*

11   *Rain Clear Cool*

**12   *Sunday Rain-Clear-Cool*
        *6 M̲o Over Sea***

Sailed   ***Hoboken***

July-   -12
            1918

13   *Rain-Clear-Cool*

**14   *Rain-Clear-Cool
        Royal Purple Bath Rob-***

15   *Rain-Clear-Cool New nurse Miss Olson Was night nurse.*

16   *Rain-Clear-Cool*

17   *Rain-Clear-Cool Service record sent to Base and disclaimed. "In France with out a Company"*

18   *Rain-Cool*

19   *Sunday Clear-1st Snow seen in France Come + gone. Read 14 letters. 200 Feeling good Y. M. S. H. is some place. Red Cross sent in magazines. Had stake*

20   *Rain-Cool   Wilcox-O'Dea-Shorty put back to company. Got out of bed for 15 min. 1st time since 31st*
Commissary Day

Chocolates	*2.65*
Stick Candy	*1.80*
Jam	*1.60*

Francis O'Dea, Co. D. Williamsport, Pennsylvania

21   *Clear-Rain   (Over-Sea)-6 Mo. Breste Bath-Pajamas Blue and Gray with R. C. Gray slipers*

22   *Clear-no rain Dinner nice stake*

23   *Clear Sharp pains not as well*

24   *Clear-Rain*

25   *Rain-Clear-Cool*

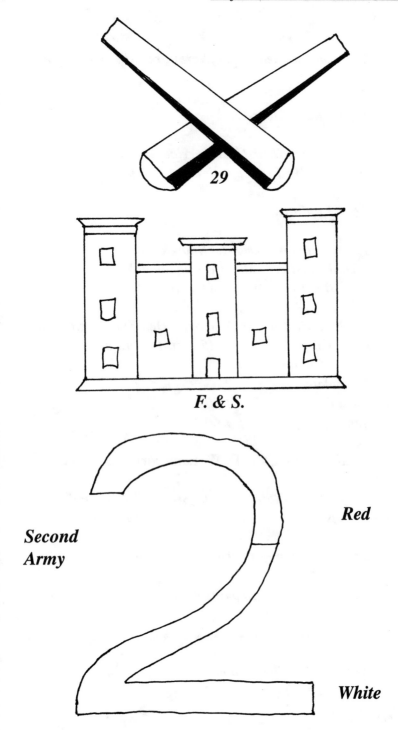

26   Sunday Clear-Rain Read things from Co.

27   Rain Cool Sgt. James came in

Adlai P. James, Co. B, Chicago, Illinois

28   Rain-Clear-Cool Got issue of clothes Got Bath 29th Eng's still at Pont R---

29   Rain-Clear-Cool

30   Clear-Rain-Cool

31   Clear-Rain

Red Cross
at
U. S. B. Hos

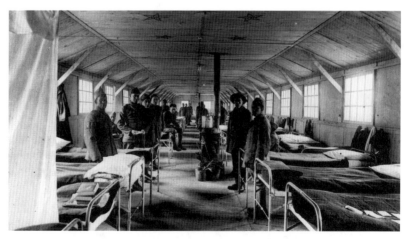

Ward #1, Medical Base Hospital No. 216, Nantes, France

Base Hospital #216--Discharge from Hospital--74th Engineers--St. Nazaire--Departure on USS Nansemond-- "?"--Summary of Dates--Rough Seas

FEBRUARY 1919

Feb.-1919   *Salary*
         28 Days $36.60

1   Clear-cool Felt better. Up all day. 32 days at Y. M. S. H.

Read letters Jan 10th addressed 74th Engineers Date of notice (12-11-18) 12-15-18. Paid-81.20 Francs-14,90 Ex. 5.45

2   Sunday Clear-Cold-Frost 74th Engs. Still at Rout - R - More of them at 216 B. H. Some in ward moved to B. H. 38 now E. H. 31

3   Cloudy-Rain-Cold Ward 17 Evacuated to Misc. Wards. Went to Ward 18. Two nurses. North and South represented.

4   Rain-Cool-Snow Ward was good but not Ward 17. We lost our Y. M. S. H. No more "Gold Bricking" a pass time at a B. H. Got new issue of clothes from bottom-out.

5   Rain-Cool-Clear Nothing extra. All is well

6   Rain-Warm All is well. Nothing extra.

7   Rain-Clear-Cold Got hair cut 2 months

8   Clear+Cold Ordered to evacuate ward 18 to ward 7 Bunch split but most all together at 7 Nurses-Miss Lockwood West Ga.
Surgical Ward #7 Alabama-paralised Case Noisy-He talked
5 Minns with Venus   Wards 6+
5 Yrs with Mercury   9

9   Sunday Clear+cold Went to Mess

10

11

12   *Co's 74th Eng's-Moved to port of Embarkation*
St. Nazaire   Had to pass to Nantes

The St. Nazaire docks

13

14

15   *Pass to Nantes*

16   *Sunday Hauleston* [Houliston] *disharged Co's*
not at Nantes
   Capt. Kleinflet [Kleinpell]*-M. C. W. S. would release*
me if Capt Pratt OK-All fixed for discharge to be sent to
company at St. Nazaire.

   Discharged from
17   ***B. H. 216***
   Rejoined 74th Eng's
   in S. O. S

*Clear+cool Departed from B H. 216 after a stay 47
days Red tape to get tickets from R. T. O.* [Railroad Transportation Officer] *Departed Class II at 9:06 Reached St Nazaire
10:36 R. T. O sent us to Camp #2 74th left for Camp #1
Isolation Sect. Reported 1:30 to C. O. 74th Eng's. Lt.
Twinham adj.* [Twynham] *Lt. Conover Person Adj played the
fancy game. Assigned to Camp Devens detachment.*

Officers of the 29th Engineers:
First Lieutenant Frank J. Twynham, El Paso, Texas
First Lieutenant Reve Conover, Oakland, California

*Busy Afternoon Visited delousing plant
Clothes sterilized Rec'd whole new out fit and Bath.
Some system U shape system. Undress on one side-every-
thing on other side*

Delousing
Signed payroll
Retired for night.
Camp #1   *-St. Nazaire*
3   *Y M C A Huts*
2   *Salvation Army Huts*
1   *K of C Hut*
2   *Red Cross Hut*
Dining Hall-8 lines
Feed 2000 every 15 minutes

American servicemen had to undergo rigorous sanitation inspections before departure from France and upon arrival to the U. S. The 1934 handbook of *Basic Field Artillery* outlined the procedures designed to rid the body of parasites:

> Vermin include lice, fleas, bed bugs and other insects. The best security against vermin is cleanliness of person, clothing and bedding. Nothing more than a bath is necessary to rid the body of fleas. Sunning and airing blankets and mattresses will usually prevent bed bugs and other insects in bedding.
>
> Lice are the insects which infest the body. They are of three varieties; the body louse or "cootie," the head louse, and the pubic louse or "crab." The *cootie* lives in clothing. It is about the size of a pin and is of dirty white color. This insect causes much suffering. During the Civil War it was known as the "greyback." Means of getting rid of the cootie are:
>
> a. By applying Heat
>
>> 1. Boil clothing for 30 minutes.
>> 2. Steam clothing, the length of time depending on the temperature.
>> 3. Press dampened clothing with a hot flat iron, especially the seams, as cooties gather and lay their eggs (nits) there.
>> 4. Hang clothing in superheated rooms (dry heat), the time depending on the temperature.
>
> Of these methods steam is the most practible where a large number of men must be taken care of. Boiling is effective, but only underclothes can be satisfactorily treated in this manner. Pressing may be used where other means are not at hand. The use of dry heat is uncertain.
>
> The "Serbian Barrel" is a simple means of destroying lice in clothing. It consists of a pan and a barrel placed over a fire. The pan contains steaming water and the barrel is perforated at the bottom, allowing steam to enter. The barrel has a tight-fitting cover. infested clothes are placed on racks in the barrel
>
> b. Chemical agents
>
>> 1. Immerse the clothing in gasoline. Bathe the body with gasoline, being careful to keep it out of eyes, mouth, rectum and genitals
>> 2. Dust vermicide powder into the clothing (1)

18 Rain-Cold Wind

19 Wed. Rain-Cool
P. S. Some one forgot to salute a major-S. O. S.-
Took Bath Major Lyman-called on carpet Repremanded with three demerits+subj. to inspections

20 Rain-Cool Co's drilled 9:30--

21 Rain-Rain Quiet Day at Isolation Camp#1

Ordered inspection	*22nd*
Medical	*23rd*
Board + Sail	*24th*

E. S.= Embarkation Service

22 Clear-Rain-Cold inspected by E. S. Major at 9:30
3-Officers of 74th Eng's attached to Casual Co #1 for sailing on Mongolia (5000)

Troops boarding the U. S. S. Mongolia at St. Nazaire, January 20, 1919

Casuals were wounded soldiers. Prior to embarkation to the U. S., disabled troops were grouped together into casual companies.

The *U. S. S. Mongolia* was an American registered transport ship. During the war, the *Mongolia* was one of the 29 ships in the New York Division of the Transport Force. It had a maximum troop-carrying capacity of 4700. In 24 voyages, the *Mongolia* successfully carried 19,013 across the Atlantic. Following the war, the *Mongolia* was officially returned to the Atlantic Transport Company on August 18, 1919.(2)

23   Sunday Rain Inspected Medical Inspection 9:30 A. M. 24 Hours before departure Full battalion in 45 minutes

24   Monday Rain-Clear-Cool Departed 10:20 P. M. Boarded Boat 4:20 U. S. S. Nansemond (German Lyde Line-Freighter Penn.) Rec'd hot chocolate from Y and Red Cross No red tape at dock.

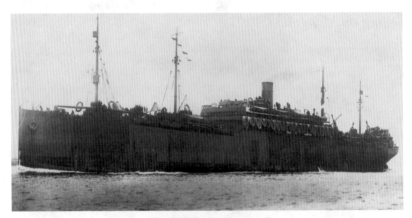

The U.S.S. Nansemond

The *U. S. S. Nansemond* was an ex-German cargo vessel formerly named the *Pennsylvania*. Displacing 27,000, the *Nansemond* was considered to be one of the largest vessels of its type in the world. The ship had a troop-carrying capacity of

5800. The _Nansemond_ was used exclusively after the war to bring American soldiers home. In five cross-Atlantic voyages, the vessel transported 23,619 troops back to the U. S. At the conclusion of its service, the _Nansemond_ remained in American hands and was transferred to the U. S. Shipping Board.(3)

?

Joli french girls, sure some of 'em
Lots "pas tou", yes most of 'em
Drink water, Hell no
    none of 'em
Use at all No tell
    by the looks of 'em
But over across the
    sea
Theres one girl I long
    to see
She came from France
    but you'll agree
She's the one best girl
    for you and me
Out in the harbor
    alone she stands
Lighting her welcome
    with outstretched hands.
She'll wait + wait
    till the world is free
Your girl - my girl,
    Miss Liberty

Composed by group of
Flash and Sound Rangers
29th Engs. Ft. St. Menge
    France

U. S. World War I Poster "Miss Liberty"

The Members of the 29th Engineers were quite adept at composing verse. In Sergeant Jesse R. Hinman's book *Ranging in France With Flash and Sound*, additional poems written by members of the 29th appear in the appendix. Here is a sampling of that work:

THE RANGERS

The Army fought its wars of old
      Without an F. and S.
Intelligence pertained to scouts,
      And guns were hit by guess.

But Uncle Sam keeps up to date,
      And seldom skips a trick,
He figured that some engineers
      Could work without a pick

The Second Battalion, 29th
      (Now in the Seventy-fourth),
Took up the work of Flash and Sound
      So feared by Ludendorf.

To map the Boche was their design,
      To ferret out his guns--
With rifles handy while they worked,
      And masks to save the lungs.

For they've held posts in the trenches,
      And even in No Man's Land.
It's well for them the tide of war
      Was toward the Vaterland.

Balloons and planes could spot by day,
      And sometimes saw the "core"
But Flash and Sound would carry on
      From "0" to "24."

On every hour of twenty-four,
      And each day of the month,

Their observers would be working
      Along the battle front.

It was no passing risk they took;
      They never got repose;
And all that kept their losses down
      Was luck, the Army knows.

They plodded steadily along,
      And won a few citations,
They put, not towns, upon the map,
      But German gun locations.

The posts were fathered by central,
      But had their "S. O. S."
Service of Salvage they called it,
      Aside from wireless.

The Boche can make good pan-cake flour,
      His jam is of the best,
And much canned milk was left behind,
      To grace the Ranger's mess.

The Sound men used to josh the Flash,
      The Flash would kid the Sound;
And often crude, or quaint remarks
      Bantered their way around.

We're fast, you're slow, declared the Flash;
      Let's call it first and second;
Four-flush and science, counterd Sound,
      Wait till results are reckoned.

They kept the gaff unto themselves,
      Nor split the hairs too fine;
For they've shared the O. P.'s together;
      They've hit the same mess line.

Our Section if the best of all,
      Was each man's open boast;
But he'd agree both Flash and Sound
      Helped rout the German host.

When history tells the war's great deeds,
    She'll make a slight digression
To teach the world that Flash and Sound
    Was more than an expression

SERGEANT FIRST CLASS HOWARD F. COLT, Co. D

A LINESMAN'S SOLILOQUY

As I sit on my bunk in my dugout,
    And it's nearly time to turn in,
With the rockets a-playing without,
    And the shrapnel's occasional "ping."

My thoughts wander back to the family,
    And out home on the side of Park Road;
And I wonder what they are doing,
    While I'm in this "classy" abode.

Perhaps they're seated at dinner,
    With tablecloth, napkins, and things
And don't have to worry about "seconds,"
    With a maid to come when they ring.

Or 'round the fire in the evening,
    With pap in his big easy chair,
And mother seated just near him,
    Oh--if I could be there.

But that is not for the present,
    For the reason we're in France,
As to breaking up family circles,
    The Hun has an execellent chance.

CORPORAL EDWARD B. SPURR, Co. D (4)

Departure for U. S. A.
on U. S. S. Nansemond
France.

July 10	*Sailed Hoboken*
1918; July 21	*Landed Breste* [Brest]
	7-Mo. 4 days in France
1919; Feb 24	*Sailed from St. Nazaire*
March 10-11	*Landed at Newport News Va.*

8 Mo Over Sea

Armistice in effect just 4 Mo today-date & hour we made port.

Feb. 1919

24   *Monday Departed Camp #1-12:30*
        Boarded Boat   4:20
U. S. S. Nansemond New York
        (N. G. Lyod Line-Freighter Penn)
        Second largest freighter afloat
        Length 670 t   Beam 63 ft
        Draw 23'-37'
        Speed 10-15 knots

25   *Named Nansemond by Mrs. Wilson-after her house in country Was formaly-Freighter Penn of Natl German Lyod Line-During war carried heavyest cargo record R. R. iron engines etc. Maned by U. S. Merchant Marine*
        On Board
                56th Engineers-1st Batt.
                53d C. A. C. 74th Art
                74th Engineers 1st Batt. 29th Engs.
                55th Supply Train

Casuals and Officers
Total 5400
Crew U. S. Navy-460

Summary of Days out
France to U. S. A.

	Feb.	24	*Boarded Boat*
		25	*Sailed 7:30 A. M.*
			Cut Loose 10:20 A. M.
	1	26	
	2	27	
	3	28	
Mar			
	4	*1*	
		2	
	5	*2*	
	6	*3*	
	7	*4*	
	8	*5*	
	9	*6*	
	10	*7*	
	11	*8*	
	12	*9*	
	12	*9*	

Mar
13   *10th*   *Sighted Light 7:30 P. M.*

        11   *Landed   1 P. M.*

Feb   *25th*   *Tuesday Rain-Clear-Cool*

            7:30   Pulled-Off
            10:20   Cut-Cast Off
            12:15   Past Outer Light
        Bay Bese   Rough and choppy
            Sailed on.

    *26th   Rain-Clear-Cool 10:20-1st Day-(24 hrs.) Out
Rough-Felt Punck-Y Poi-Bon on Board Treatment Casuals
punck Sea High*

    *27   Rain-Clear-Cool Hit Storm at night 2 Boats
past on Port Sick Bunch Bow plunged 20± feet Some ride-
Slept on table Leviathan past on Port Side*

    *28   Clear-Warm 2 Meals not enough Inlisted men
to crowded 300 inlisted of 5500 better Sea Quiet*
        10:20 End of 3d̲ Day.

At Sea--Arrived at Newport News--Camp Stuart--Major Lyman's Final Address--Camp Upton, Long Island-- Discharge

MARCH 1919

March. 1919

*1   Sat. Clear-Warm   Sea running high 2:05 St.
Nazaire-12:00 at Sea*

*2   Sunday   Rain-Cold-Storm-N. E. Rolling
mountains of water Warning Read from Leviathan
Mongolia hit hard 2:28 St N.-12:00 at Sea*

*3   Clear-Glorious-Warm-N. W. Rolling Sea but
stormed part-12 Noon*
         Log. 42-30'   Lat
         3:05 St N.   12:00 at Sea

*4   Clear-Cloudy-Cool-S. W. wind 70 mile gale
Sea chopy+rolling*
         Log.   Lat.
         Dist 1572   Course

*5   High Sea-Storm S. W. 60 mile gale Rain-Cold
Sailor Shot*
     "   fell out crows nest
Dist to go 1352 Cape Henry
3:40 St. N   12:00 Sea

*6   Cloudy-Clear-Calm Sea-N. E. Hit Gulf Stream
2:30 Warm Had Eggs-first pick up on food*
         4:00 St. N-   12:00 Sea

*7   Cloudy-Warm Calm Sea N. W. Very Quiet
10:20 A. M.-10 days out*
4:15 St N.-12:00 Sea

*8   Sat Cloudy-Warm-Calm Sea-N. E. Orders to
follow orders of port cleared for New Port News. Va.*
         Dist off Cape henry 572 miles noon

9

9th   Sunday Clear-Cloudy-N. E. Heavy Gale at 4 P, M. throu out night. Raving Sea.

572

10th   Clear-Cold Sea ran high till noon-thru calm as lamb Made fine time

43-0'   73-0'

Dest 10 miles   12:00

Reached Cape Henry Light Ship 7:30 P. M. Took orders and drifted for night with a quiet sea.

11th   Clear-cool Sailed on at 6:00 A. M. Sighted first land 7:30 Sailed up Chespeake Bay. Took on pilot at 8:10 Docked at 11:00
       74th U. S. Eng's-Led by two bands paraded to camp. Royal reception by people of NewPort News Va.
       Cheese sandwiches-chocolate-cookies-cigaretts on Landing Red Cross etc.
       Women of Newport cup cakes, fruit, gum, flowers, fudge
       Camped at Camp Stuart Big Camp. Fine canteen service. Fine ice cream first in eight months
       Meet off Fortress Monroe by Ship Relief with Reception Committee. Hydro-plane above while band played.

A *Newport News Times-Herald* article highlighted the arrival of the *Nansemond* to port in Newport News, Virginia on March 11:

LARGEST SHIP WITH LARGEST GANG ON, HERE

U.S.S. Nansemond, carrying 5,427 Men Turn Loose Rampant Warriors for
Camps This Afternoon--Morrison and Naval Transport Bands Play

---

With two brass bands, that from camp Morrison and the
Naval Transport band, playing martial melodies, the largest
number of soldiers paraded from the largest troopship to arrive
here, through the streets of the city this afternoon at about 1:15
o'clock.

The U. S. S. Nansemond arrived in harbor from St.
Nazaire, France early this morning and docked shortly before
noon. She had aboard 5,437 men, representing every State in the
Union and many of the "outfits" overseas. All were happy as
larks.

Aboard the Nansemond were the Seventy-fourth
engineers, the Fifty-third heavy artillery, the Fifty-sixth engineers,
the Fifty-fifth ammunition train, a cement mill company for Camp
Meade, and nine casual companies from Ohio, Iowa, Kentucky,
Arkansas, Colorado, Illinois, and Wisconsin. The casuals were
placed in motor trucks and carried to Camp Hill.

Troops aboard stated though they were in cramped
quarters, the Nansemond rode a stormy voyage in good fashion.
However, they were glad to look upon the shore this morning.
From every port hole a hand extended; the decks were a dull
brown, and even the rigging seemed to be alive with warriors of
Verdun and St. Mihiel.

Members of the Seventy-fourth engineers stated they
were one battalion of the old Twenty-ninth engineers, the only
flash and sound ranging outfit overseas. Their work was to
detect the enemy guns by triangulation. They operated from
Verdun and Metz, and participated in much of the hardest fighting.
They were from all parts of America. Members of the heavy
artillery outfit, commanded by Colonel Gregg, are from the West.
They were trained at the Presidio, in California. Many of the boys
in the Fifty-fifth ammunition train are from Los Angeles.

All along the line of march today different citizens
rushed out and feverishly distributed chocolate, oranges, snacks
and other delicacies.

"We can read the signs on the buildings, eh?"
"I can say, is this a dry town, or what is it?"

"Here, take this gun; I'm through with it."

"When do we eat?" and other snappy phrases were tossed out by the hilarious home comers.

Lee Turner, of this city, who was employed at the customs house prior to joining the army, came back with the Seventy-fourth engineers.1

Life back in

U. S. A.

Camp Stuart
  Newport News Va   March 11th to 17th
Camp Upton

March 1919

11   Tuesday
    Landed and settled in Camp Stuart Va,
    De-Cootyized at 8:45 P. M. and we came out
pure.

12   Clear-warm
    Quarantine Lifted at 3:00 P. M.
    Artillary Co's come in 26 days out on U. S.
Battleship Ohio from Brest. Sent Packages

13   Clear Warm
    Issue of clothes etc Quiet day
    A chosen--bunch in 17 days Anhirs.

14   Cloudy-Clar-Cool-Rain
    Inspection by Camp Stuart Command
    4 Embarcation Service

15   Clear-Warm   Final wind up

> *16   Sunday*
> *Clear-Warm*
> *Revealry   7:15*
> *Breakfast   7:30*
> *Ralla*
>
> *Presented Capt. Wright-F. R. S. #2 with Hamilton Watch. ap*
> *Replied briefly saying he didn't receive any D. S. C. or such but he had received what he valued as highly now and he was confident that squareness in a walk of life makes success. Capt. Wright C. O. of F R S #1 & #2*

On March 16, Major Theodore Lyman addressed members of the 29th Engineers for the last time.

> *Battalion Assembled by Major at 1:00 P. M.*
> *Battalion Attention*
> *Men this is the last time we will exist united as a battalion of old 29th new 74th Engineers. It has been a great pleasure to be associated with you and command you. Your part in the big struggle has been nobley and honorably filled. Your work not known to the public as well as divisions but is found on the timely sheets of the records of the A. E. F.-->*
> *Now as you enter civilian life once more may you carry with it the high personal and same success you have achieved as members of the Army Observation Corp. 74th Eng's*
> *At Ease--*

> *Final Division of Battalions for Misc. Camps*

I	*Camp Devens*	*-Lt. Church*
*	*Camp Upton*	*-Lt. Monk-Smith*
	Camp Meade	
	Camp Dix	*Capt. Wright*

> _II_   _Camp Fremont_
>   _Camp Custer_
>   _Camp Houston_
>   _Camp Grant_
>   _Camp Jefferson_

Once the 74th Engineers was officially dissolved, the members of its two battalions were transported by train to camps near their homes for discharge. Individuals in the First Battalion were sent to Camp Devens, Ayer, Massachusetts; Camp Upton, Long Island, New York; Camp Meade, Baltimore, Maryland; and Camp Dix, New Jersey. Troops in the Second Battalion were discharged at Camp Freemont, Palo Alto, California; Camp Custer, Battle Creek, Michigan; Fort Sam Houston, Houston, Texas; Camp Grant, Rockford, Illinois; and Jefferson Barracks, St. Louis, Missouri.

Officers of the 29th Engineers:
First Lieutenant Sanford E. Church, Cleveland, Ohio
First Lieutenant Percy S. Monk, Sleansville, New York
Second Lieutenant Merril J. Smith, Carsadaga. New York

Camp Stuart Newport News Va
>   _to Camp Upton Long Island_

> _17th_   _Monday_
>   _Revealry_   _5:00_
>   _Breakfast_   _5:30_
>   _Assembly_   _6:30_
> _Detachment II left at 11:00 A, M. for west_
> _Detachment I delaid because of cars off track and tigh_

_up._
>   _Left 7:20_
>   _Richmond Va 10:30 P. M._
>   _Washington D. C._

18th

Washington D. C.	*1:20 A. M*
North Phil	*7:20*
N.Y. Penn Sta	*12:30*
Jamaica L. I.	*2:30 P. M.*
Switched	
Camp Upton	*6:50 P. M.*

Remarks on trip

"Y" *on board with cigaretts chocolate-matches and games*

Red Cross

Chocolate Hot-buns-cookies-cigaretts apples at Richmond Va.

Milk Can Coffee-buns apple cakes put on at North Phil. Pa.

Hot Chocolate-buns apples, cigaretts, sandwiches

Attached to:--

8 Co-2nd Batt. 152 Depot Brigade Camp Upton L. I. for discharge.

Camp Upton

30 wks.

19th   Lecture at 9:30

U. S. Army-Compensation + Employment

Medical Exam 2:30

20 Doctors-Some different than gong in

Remarks:--

20th

> *Called in Equipment*
> *Called for Final papers*
> *Signed Discharge*
> *Complete at 4:35 P. M.*

21th

22nd   *Sat March 1919*

       Discharged.

Bristol City Engineer Clair M. Pfennig, July 1941

One of the more disappointing aspects concerning my research of Clair Pfennig was my inability to secure a wartime photograph of him. The only image I was able to locate was this
copy of a photograph taken from a scrapbook. Bristol librarian
Ruth Dittman found it. The fact that Mr. Pfennig and his wife
were childless made any attempt to locate living family nearly
impossible. I contacted the University of Connecticut to inquire
about a yearbook picture. Unfortunately, his attendance pre-dated
the custom of producing such a book. Efforts to locate a wartime
photo through the National Archives, the Connecticut State Archives, the U. S. Army and the American Legion did not turn up
a single picture. All that I can say is that somewhere on that
cover photograph, among the troops of the 74th Engineers, is
Private Clair M. Pfennig, Flash Ranger, A.E.F.

APPENDIX

CONDITIONS OF AN ARMISTICE WITH GERMANY

A. Military clauses on western front

1. Cessation of operations by land and in the air six hours after the signature of the armistice.

2. Immediate evacuation of invaded countries: Belgium, France, Alsace Lorraine, Luxembourg, so ordered as to be completed within 14 days from the signature of the armistice.

German troops which have not left the above-mentioned territories within the period fixed will become prisoners of war.

Occupation by the Allied and United States forces jointly will keep pace with evacuation in these areas.

All movements of evacuation and occupation will be regulated in accordance with a note (annexure 1).

3. Repatriation, beginning at once, to be completed within 14 days, of all inhabitants of the countries above enumerated (including hostages, persons under tiral or convicted).

4. Surrender in good condition by the German armies of the following equipment:

> 5,000 guns (2,500 heavy, 2,500 field)
> 30,000 machine guns
> 3,000 *minewerfer*
> 2,000 aeroplanes (fighters, bombers--firstly D.7's--and
> > night bombing machines

The above to be delivered *in situ* to the Allied and United States troops in accordance with the detailed conditions laid down in note (annexure 1).

5. Evacuation by the German armies of the countries on the left bank of the Rhine. These countries on the left bank of the Rhine shall be administered by the local authorities under the

control of the Allied and United States armies of occupation.

The occupation of these territories will be carried out by Allied and United States garrisons holding the principal crossings of the Rhine (Mayence, Coblenz, Cologne) together with bridgeheads at these points of a 30-kilometer radius on the right bank and by garrisons similarly holding the strategic points of the regions.

A neutral zone shall be reserved on the right bank of the Rhine between the stream and a line drawn parallel to a 40 kilometers to the east from the frontier of Holland to the parallel of Gernsheim and at a distance of 30 kilometers only east of the stream from this parallel up to the Swiss frontier.

Evacuation by the enemy of the Rhinelands shall be so ordered as to be completed within a further period of 11 days, in all, 25 days after the signature of the armistice.

All movements of evacuation and occupation will be regulated according to the note (annexure 1).

6. In all territory evacuated by the enemy there shall be no evacuation of inhabitants; no damage or harm shall be done to persons or property of the inhabitants.

No destruction of any kind committed.

Military establishments of all kinds shall be delivered intact, as well as military stores of food, munitions, equipment not removed during the periods fixed for evacuation.

Stores of food of all kinds for the civil population, cattle, etc., shall be left *in situ.*

Industrial establishments shall not be impaired in any way and their personnel shall not be moved.

7. Roads and means of communication of every kind, railroads, waterways, main roads, bridges, telegraphs, telephones, shall be in no matter impaired.

All civil and military personnel at present employed on them shall remain.

5,000 locomotives, 150,000 wagons and 10,000 motor lorries in good working order with all necessary spare parts and fittings shall be delivered to the Associated Powers within the period fixed for the evacuation of Belgium and Luxemburg.

The railways of Alsace-Lorraine shall be handed over within the same period together with all pre-war personnel and material.

Further, the material necessary for the working of railways in the country on the left bank of the Rhine shall be left *in situ.*

All stores of coal and material for upkeep of permanent way, signals, and repair shops shall be left *in situ* and kept in an efficient state by Germany during the whole period of the armistice.

All barges taken from the Allies shall be restored to them: the note appended as annexure 2 regulates the detail of these measures.

8. The German Command shall be responsible for revealing all mines or delay action fuses disposed on territory evacuated by the German troops and shall assist in their discovery and destruction.

The German Command shall also reveal all destructive measures that may have been taken (such as poisoning or pollution of springs, wells, etc.), under penalty of reprisals.

9. The right of requisition shall be exercised by the Allied and United States armies in all occupied territory.

The upkeep of the troops of occupation in the Rhineland (excluding Alsace-Lorraine) shall be charged to the German Government.

10. The immediate repatriation, without reciprocity, according to detailed conditions which shall be fixed, of all Allied and United States prisoners of war. The Allied Powers and the United States prisoners of war. The Allied Powers and the United States of America shall be able to dispose of these prisoners as they wish.

11. Sick and wounded who cannot be removed from evacuated territory will be cared for by German personnel who will be left on the spot with the medical material required.

B. Dispositions relative to the eastern frontiers of Germany

12. All German troops at present in any territory which before the war belonged to Russia, Roumania, or Turkey shall withdraw within the frontiers of Germany as they existed on August 1, 1914.

13. Evacuation by German troops to begin at once and all German instructors, prisoners, and civilians as well as military agents now on the territory of Russia (as defined on August 1, 1914) to be recalled.

14. German troops to cease at once all requisitions and seizures and any other undertaking with a view to obtaining supplies intended for Germany in Roumania and Russia (as defined on August 1, 1914)

15. Abandonment of the treaties of Bucharest and Brest-Litovsk and of supplementary treaties.

16. The Allies shall have free access to the territories evacuated by the Germans on their eastern frontier, either through Danzig or by the Vistula, in order to convey supplies to the populations of those territories or for any other purpose.

C. Clause concerning East Africa

17. Unconditional capitulation of all German forces operating in East Africa, within one month.

D. General Clauses

18. Repatriation, without reciprocity, within a maximum period of one month, in accordance with detailed conditions hereafter to be fixed, of all civilians interned or deported who may be citizens of other Allied or Associated states than those mentioned in clause 3.

19. With the reservation that any future claims and demands of the Allies and United States of America remain unaffected, the following financial conditions are required:

Reparation for damage done.

While the armistice lasts no public securities shall be removed by the enemy which can serve as a pledge to the Allies for the recovery or reparation for war losses.

Immediate restitution of the cash deposit in the National Bank of Belgium and, in general, immediate return of all documents, specie, stock, shares, paper money together with plant for the issue thereof, touching public or private interests in the invaded countries.

Restitution of the Russian and Roumanian gold yielded to Germany or taken by that power.

This gold to be delivered in trust to the Allies until signature of peace.

E. Naval conditions

20. Immediate cessation of all hostilities at sea and definite information to be given as to the location and movements of all German ships.

Notification to be given to neutrals that freedom of navigation in all territorial waters is given to the naval and mercantile marines of the Allied and Associated Powers in German hands to be returned, without reciprocity.

21. All naval and mercantile marine prisoners of war of the Allied and Associated Powers in German hands to be returned, without reciprocity.

22. Surrender to the Allies and the United States of America of 160 German submarines (including all submarine cruisers and minelaying submarines) with their complete armament and equipment, in ports which will be specified by the Allies and the United States of America. All other submarines to be paid off and completely disarmed and placed under the supervision of the Allies and the United States of America.

23. The following German surface warships, which shall be designated by the Allies and the United States of America, shall forthwith be disarmed and thereafter interned in neutral ports to be designated by the Allies and the United States of America, and placed under the surveillance of the Allies and the United States of America, only caretakers being left on board, namely:

> 6 battle cruisers
> 10 battleships
> 8 light cruisers, including 2 mine layers
> 50 destroyers of the most modern types

All other surface warships (including river craft) are to be concentrated in German naval bases to be designated by the Allies and the United States of America, and are to be paid off and completely disarmed and placed under the supervision of the Allies and the United States of America. All vessels of the auxiliary fleet (trawlers, motor vessels, etc.)are to be disarmed.

24. The Allies and the United States of America shall have the right to sweep up all mine fields and obstructions laid by Germany outside German territorial waters, and the positions of these are to be indicated.

25. Freedom of access to and from the Baltic to be given to the naval and mercantile marines of the Allied and Associated Powers. To secure this the Allies and the United States of America shall be empowered to occupy all German forts, fortifications, batteries and defense works of all kinds in all the entrances from the Cattegat into the Baltic, and to sweep up all mines and obstructions within and without German territorial waters without any questions of neutrality being raised, and the positions of all such mines and obstructions are to be indicated.

26. The existing blockade conditions set up by the Allied and Associated Powers are to remain unchanged, and all German merchant ships found at sea are to remain liable to capture.

27. All naval aircraft are to be concentrated and immobilized in German bases to be specified by the Allies and the United States of America.

28. In evacuating the Belgian coasts and ports, Germany shall abandon all merchant ships, tugs, lighters, cranes and all other harbor materials, all materials for inland navigation, all aircraft and air materials and stores, all arms and armaments, and all stores and apparatus of all kinds.

29. All Black Sea ports are to be evacuated by Germany; all Russian warships of all descriptions seized by Germany in the Black Sea are to be handed over to the Allies and the United States of America; all neutral merchant ships seized are to be released; all warlike and other materials of all kinds seized in those ports are to be returned and German materials as specified in clause 28 are to be abandoned.

30. All merchant ships in German hands belonging to the Allied and Associated Powers are to be restored in ports to be specified by the Allies and the United States of Americas without reciprocity.

31. No destruction of ships or of materials to be permitted before evacuation, surrender or restoration.

32. The German Government shall formally notify the neutral governments of the world, and particularly the Governments of Norway, Sweden, Denmark, and Holland, that all restrictions placed on the trading of their vessels with the Allied and Associated countries, whether in return for specific concessions such as the export of shipbuilding materials or not, are immediately canceled.

33. No transfers of German merchant shipping of any description to any neutral flag are to take place after the signature of the armistice.

F. Duration of armistice

34. The duration of the armistice is to be 30 days, with option to extend. During this period, on failure of execution of any of the above clauses, the armistice may be denounced by one of the contracting parties, on 48 hours' previous notice.

G. *Time limit for reply*

35. This armistice to be accepted or refused by Germany within 72 hours of notification.

NOTES

MAY 1918

1. John J. Pershing, Commander-in-Chief, American Expedition-
ary Forces, *My Experiences in the World War, Volume I*, (New York:
Fredderick A. Stokes Company, 1931), pp. 14 and 20-22 and Daniel J.
Boorstin and Brooks Mather Kelly, *A History of the United States*,
(Englewood Cliffs, N. J.: Prentice-Hall, Inc., 1990), p. 466.

2. Pershing, *Volume I,* pp. 280-282.

3. *Order of Battle of the United States Land Forces in the World
War (1917-19), Zone of the Interior, Directory of Troops, Volume III, Part
2,*(Washington, D.C.: United States Army War College--United States
Printing Office, 1949), pp. 177 and 187.

JUNE 1918

1. Pershing, *Volume II*, p. 125.

2. *The Bristol Press*, (September 13, 1888).

3. Sergeant Jesse R. Hinman, *Ranging in France with Flash and
Sound*, (Portland, Oregon: Press of Dunham Printing Company, 1919),
p. 25.

JULY 1918

1. *The Washington Post,* (July 5, 1918), pp. 2 and 12.

2. *The Washington Post*, (July 8, 1918), p. 4.

3. *Order of Battle of the United States Land Forces in the World War (1917-1919), Zone of the Interior, War Department; Territorial Departments; Tactical Divisions; Posts, Camps, and Stations, Volume II, Part I,* (Washington D.C.: United States Army War College--United States Printing Office, 1949), pp. 512-517.

4. John H. Melville, *The Great White Fleet,* (New York: Vantage Press, 1976), pp.95-103 and *Order of Battle . . ., Volume III, Part I,* p. 510.

5. Vice Admiral Albert Gleaves, U.S.N., *A History of the Transport Service,* (New York: George H. Doran Company,1921), pp. 82-83.

6. Gleaves, p. 84.

7. Samuel L. A. Marshall, *World War I,* (New York: American Heritage Publishing Co., Inc., 1964), pp. 341-416 and Pershing, *Volume I,* pp. 53-191.

8. John Dos Passos, *Mr Wilson's War,* (London: Hamish Hamilton, 1962), pp. 228-242 and Gleaves, pp. 166-171.

9. Dos Passos, pp. 228-242.

10. Pershing, *Volume I,* p. 87.

11. Gleaves, p. 25.

12. Ibid., p. 25

13. Ibid., pp. 26 and 64.

14. Ibid., p. 143.

15. Ibid., p. 82.

16. Ibid., p. 42.

17. *Order of Battle . . ., Volume III, Part I,* p. 508 and Gleaves, pp. 68-69 and 188-189.

18. Lewis P. Clephane, *History of the Naval Overseas Transportation Service in World War I,* (Washington D.C.:Naval History Division, 1969), pp. viii and 143.

19. *Order of Battle . . ., Volume III, Part 1*, p. 505.

20. Pershing, *Volume II*, p. 200.

21. Pershing, *Volume II*, p. 201 and William L. Langer, *Gas and Flame in World War I*, (New York: Alfred Knopff, Inc., 1965), p. 13.

22. Pershing, *Volume I*, p. 127.

23. Henry Berry, *Make the Kaiser Dance*, (New York: Priam Books, 1978), p. 107 and Pershing, *Volume II*, p. 56.

24. Hinman, pp. 235-236.

25. Marshall, p. 43.

26. Maurice Francis Egan and John B. Kennedy, *The Knights of Columbus in Peace and War, Volume I*, (New Haven, CT: The Knights of Columbus, 1920), pp. 252-253 and Pershing, *Volume I*, pp. 35, 71-74 and 107-108.

27. Barry, p. 154.

28. *Order of Battle of the United States Land Forces in the World War, American Expeditionary Forces, Divisions, Volume II*, (Washington, D.C.: United States Army War College--United States Printing Office, 1949), p. 275 and Barry, pp. 307-308.

29. Frank E. Vandiver, Black Jack: *The Life and Times of John J. Pershing, Volumes I and II*, (College Station, Texas: Texas A&M University Press, 1977) and Marshall, pp. 270-271.

AUGUST 1918

1. Pershing, *Volume I*, pp. 150-156

2. Joseph T. Dickman, Major General, American Army, Commanding Third Army, *The Great Crusade*, (New York: D. Appleton and Company, 1927), pp. 36-39 and 46.

3. Hinman, p. 17.

4. *Summary of World War Work of the American Y.M.C.A,*

(The International Committee of Young Men's Christian Associations, 1920), p.120.

    5. Pershing, _Volume II_, pp. 236-237.

    6. Ibid., p. 213.

    7. Hinman, p. 20-21.

    8. Richard Goldhurst, _The Midnight War_, (New York: McGraw-Hill Co., 1978), W. Bruce Lincoln, _Red Victory, A History of the Russian Civil War_, (New York: Simon and Schuster, 1989), pp. 163-165, and John Toland, _No Man's Land_, (Garden City, New York: Doubleday and Co., 1980), pp. 385-405.

    9. Benedict Crowell, _America's Munitions 1917-1918_, (Washington, D.C.: U.S. War Department, Government Printing Office, 1919), pp. 401-405 and Marshall, pp. 157 and 163-166.

    10. Hinman, pp. 213-223.

SEPTEMBER 1918

    1. Ibid., pp. 199-212.

    2. _Handbook of Artillery_, (Washington, D.C.: Office of the Chief of Ordnance, Government Printing Office, 1920), pp. 80-93, Henry A. Benwell, _History of the Yankee Division_, (Boston: The Cornhill Company, 1919), pp. 43-44, Curt Johnson, _Artillery_, (London: Octopus Books, 1975), pp. 50-51, Crowell, p. 40, and Pershing, _Volume II_, pp. 106-107.

    3. Pershing, _Volume I_, p. 177.

    4. Gleaves, pp. 143-153.

    5. Crowell, Figure 1, p. 27.

    6. George C. Marshall, _Memoirs of My Services in the World War 1917-1918_, (Boston: Houghton-Mifflin Company, 1976), pp. 131-147, Pershing, _Volume I_, pp. 83-86 and _Volume II_, pp. 259-275, and Marshall, pp. 421-426.

7. *Summary of World War Work of the American Y.M.C.A.*, pp. 125-131.

8. Pershing, *Volume II*, p. 327.

9. Hinman, pp. 26-27.

10. Pershing, *Volume I*, pp. 128-129.

11. *Order of Battle of the United States Land Forces in the World War, American Expeditionary Forces, Divisions*.

12. Hinman, p. 16.

13. Ian V. Hogg, *The Guns 1914-18*, (New York: Ballantine Books Inc., 1971), pp. 10-43 and Kenneth Allen, *Big Guns of the Twentieth Century and Their Part in Great Battles*, (East Sussex, Great Britain: Firefly Books, 1976), pp. 18-23.

14. Hinman, pp. 157-185.

15. Guido Rosignoli, *Army Patches and Insignia Since 1939, Omnibus Edition*, (Poole, Dorset: Blandford Press, 1972), pp. 197-199 and Plate 68.

16. Aaron Norman, *The Great Air War*, (New York: The Macmillan Company, 1968), pp. 1-11 and 485-508 and Lt. Lucien H. Thayer, Edited by Donald J. McGee and Roger J. Bender, *America's First Eagles: The Official History of the U.S. Air Service, A.E.F. (1917-1918)*, (San Jose, California and Mesa, Arizona: R. James Bender Publishing and Champlin Fighter Museum Press, 1983), pp. 9-40. Lee Kennett, *The First Air War, 1914-1918*, (New York: The Free Press, 1991) provides an excellent overview of the entire war in the air.

17. Pershing, *Volume II*, pp. 317-318.

18. Carter H. Harrison, Captain A.R.C., *With the American Red Cross in France 1918-1919*, (New York: Ralph Fletcher Seymour Publisher, 1947), pp. 32-42.

19. Ibid., p. 127.

20. Hinman, p. 201.

21. Ibid., pp. 199-200.

22. Pershing, *Volume II*, p. 221.

23. Brigadier-General William Mitchell, *Memoirs of World War I*, (New York: Random House, 1956), p. 180.

OCTOBER 1918

1. Hinman, pp. 200-204.

2. Ibid., pp. 205-206.

3. John Keegan, *The Face of Battle*, (New York: Viking Press, 1976), p. 217, Jay M. Lee, *The Artilleryman*, (Kansas City, Missouri: Spencer Printing Company, 1920), p. 325, and Arthur R. Wilson, *Field Artillery Manual, Volume II*, (Menasha, Wisconsin: George Banta Publishing Company, 1929), pp. 246-261.

4. J. M. Winter, *The Experience of World War I*, (New York: Oxford University Press, 1989), p. 138 and Johnson, pp. 49-52.

5. *Notes on German Shells*, (London: General Staff (Intelligence), General Headquarters, 1918), p. 25 and Hinman, *Ranging in France With Flash and Sound.*

6. Kennett, pp. 23-40 and Crowell, pp. 331-335.

7. John Terraine, *To Win a War,* (Garden City, New York: Doubleday & Company, Inc., 1981), pp. 156-210, Leon H. Canfield, *The Presidency of Woodrow Wilson*, (Rutherford, New Jersey: Farleigh Dickinson University Press, 1966), pp. 132-142, and Marshall, pp. 431-447.

8. Hinman, pp. 157-185.

9. Evangeline Booth and Grace Livingstone Hill, *The War Romance of the Salvation Army*, (Philadelphia: J. B. Lippincott Company, 1919), pp. 226.

10. Berry, p. 13.

11. *Notes on German Shells*, pp. 142-145 and 468-469.

12. Ibid., pp. 150-179, 188-203, 472-473, and 480-487 and Winter, p. 138.

13. *USAF Historical Study no. 133, U. S. Air Service Victory Credits, World War I*, (Maxwell Air Force Base, Alabama: Historical Research Division, U. S. Aerospace Studies Institute, Air University 1969), pp. 1-4, Kennett, p. 164, Thayer, p. 315, and Aaron Norman, *The Great Air War*, (New York: The Macmillan Company, 1968), p.2.

14. Pershing, *Volume II*, pp. 130-132 and Berry, p. 438.

15. Johnson, p. 135 and Hogg, p. 25.

16. *German Shells*, pp. 45-52 and 385-386.

17. Marshall, pp. 431-435, Terraine, pp. 156-163, Canfield, pp. 132-134, and *Papers Relating to the Foreign Relations of the United States, 1918, Supplement 1, The World War, Volume I*, (Washington D.C.: The United States Government Printing Office, 1933), pp. 338 and 343.

18. *Handbook of Ordnance Data, November 15, 1918*, (Washington, D.C.: Government Printing Office, 1919), pp. 120-121.

19. Crowell, p. 474.

20. Pershing, *Volume II*, pp. 294-387 and Marshall, pp. 426-431 and pp. 438-443.

21. Terraine, pp. 176-178, Canfield, pp. 134-136, Marshall, p. 436, and *Papers Relating to the Foreign Relations of the United States, 1918, Supplement 1, The World War, Volume I*, pp. 357-359.

22. Hogg, p. 89.

23. Terraine, pp. 186-192, Canfield p. 136, Marshall, p. 436 and *Papers Relating to the Foreign Relations of the United States 1918, Suplement 1, The World War, Volume I*, pp. 380-381.

24. *Handbook of Ordnance Data, November 15, 1918*, pp. 26 and 88-107.

25. *Papers Relating to the Foreign Relations of the United Sates 1918, Supplement 1, The World War, Volume I*, pp. 381-383.

26. Crowell, pp. 75-79, _Handbook of Artillery_, pp. 211-213, and _Handbook of the 155m/m Schneider Howitzers_, (Washington, D. C.: Office C. O. O., American E. F. F. A. Section, 1918).

27. Crowell, pp. 84-90.

28. Terraine, pp. 198-200, Marshall, p. 441, and _Papers Relating to the Foreign Relations of the United States, Supplement 1, The World War, Volume I_, pp. 395-396.

29. Hinman, p. 163.

30. _Papers Relating to the Foreign Policy of the United States 1918, Supplement 1, The World War, Volume I_, pp. 404-405.

NOVEMBER 1918

1. _Order of Battle of the United States Land Forces in the World War, American Expeditionary Forces, Volume II_, pp. 38-39, 76-77, and 103.

2. _Papers Relating to the Foreign Policy of the United States 1918, Supplement 1, The World War, Volume I_, pp. 441-443.

3. Booth and Hill, pp. 75-78.

4. _Papers Relating to the Foreign Relations of the United States 1918, Supplement 1, The World War, Volume I_, pp. 433-435 and 447.

5. _Order of Battle of the United States Land Forces in the World War, American Expeditionary Forces, Divisions, Volume II_, pp. 98-105.

6. Hinman, pp. 43-48.

7. _USAF Historical Study No. 133, U.S. Air Service Victory Credits, World War I_, pp. 112-113 and Thayer, pp. 26, 230, and 346.

8. Ferdinad Foch, _The Memoirs of Marshal Foch_, (New York: Doubleday, Doran and Co., 1931), p. 466.

9. Hogg, p. 136 and _Notes on German Shells_, p. 338.

10. Foch, p. 468.

11. Marshall, p. 445 and Terraine, pp. 221-228.

12. Thayer, pp. 296 and 313-314.

13. Foch, pp. 467-487.

14. Hinman, pp. 228-229.

15. Pershing, *Volume I*, pp. 88-89.

16. *Annual Report of the Adjutant-General of the State of New York For the Year 1901,* (Albany: J. B. Lyon Company, State Printers, 1902) and the *Official Mustering Papers of Harvey J. Merchant.*

17. *Order of Battle of the United States Land Forces in the World War, American Expeditionary Forces, General Headquarters, Armies, Army Corps, Services of Supply and Separate Forces,* pp. 269-289.

18. Crowell, p. 102.

19. Hinman, pp. 229-230.

20. Ibid., pp. 180-181.

21. *Order of Battle of the United States Land Forces in the World War, Volume II, American Expeditionary Forces, Divisions,* p. 272.

22. *Order of Battle of the United States Land Forces in the World War, American Expeditionary Forces, General Headquarters, Armies, Army Corps, Services of Supply, and Separate Forces,* pp. 170-171 and 268-69.

23. Hinman, pp. 181-182.

24. Terraine, pp. 120-122.

25. Barry, pp. 271-272.

26. Hinman, pp. 182-183.

27. Ibid.

DECEMBER 1918

1. Hinman, pp. 183-185.

2. *Development of the Field Artillery Observation (Target Acquisition) Battalions, Handout,* (Fort Sill, Oklahoma: U. S. Army Field Artillery School, Target Acqusition Department, 1972), pp. 10-14 and Hinman, pp. 15-16.

3. Hinman, p. 234.

4. Arthur E. Barbeau and Florette Henri, *The Unkown Soldiers: Black American Troops in World War I,* (Philadelphia: Temple University Press, 1974), pp. 6-11 and 137-163, *Order of Battle of the United States Land Forces in the World War, Volume II, American Expeditionary Forces, Divisions,* pp. 428-435, and Mitchell, p. 291.

5. Pershing, *Volume I,* pp. 199-200.

JANUARY 1919

1. Major General M. W. Ireland, T*he Medical Department of the United States Army in the World War, Volume II, Administration American Expeditionary Forces,* (Washington, D.C.:United States Government Printing Office, 1927), p. 745.

FEBRUARY 1919

1. *Basic Field Artillery*, (Washington, D. C.: Military Service Publishing Company, 1934), p. 94.

2. Gleaves, pp. 240 and 248-249.

3. Ibid., pp. 258-259.

4. Hinman, pp. 239-249.

MARCH 1919

1. *The Newport News Times-Herald*, March 11, 1919, p. 2.

ACKNOWLEDGEMENTS

I would like to thank the many people who assisted me in putting together this book. First of all, I thank my mother-in-law Carol Datuin. Had it not been for her curiosity at that antique store in Connecticut, I would have never had had access to such an interesting primary document as Private Pfennig's diary. Second of all, I am appreciative of the assistance given to me by Ruth Dittman of the Bristol Public Library. With initials I was able to provide her, she helped me pinpoint the author of the diary. She also sent me valuable information about Clair Pfennig's background and family history.

I am also indebted to the many people who helped me with my research. The staff of the St. Louis Public Library, especially Edward Cook, provided me with many relevant sources from their own holdings and from inter-library loan. The following people, organizations, and institutions all provided invaluable information for which I am grateful: Office of the Adjutant General, Military Department of the State of Connecticut; Frank Braynard, Merchant Marine historian; the American Merchant Marine Museum; Seichepray Post #2, American Legion, Bristol; the University of Connecticut; Office of the Adjutant General, State of Rhode Island; U. S. Army Military History Institute, Carlisle Barracks; Military Records Section, Commonwealth of Massachusetts; the National War College; Office of History, U. S. Army Corps of Engineers; the Connecticut State Library; and the National Archives and Records Administration. The Photographic Division of the National Archives was extremely helpful with regards to the acquisition of photographs.

A couple of people in particular provided invaluable assistance when it came to the actual mechanics of creating this book. Marty McCabe, a teaching colleague, provided me with insight on word processing and layout. His son Jerry McCabe created the cover. Father Ralph Wright, O.S.B., a published poet himself, gave me some good advice. Tom Pulliam, a longtime friend, shared his business expertise. My mother, Barbara Finan, acted as an editorial critic of my original manuscript. Her incredible eye and ear for the English language was a tremendous aid to my writing. My brothers Mike and Tom gave me tips on a whole host of topics, from desktop publishing to photography to history. My father-in-law, Dr. Alex Datuin, provided photographic equipment. I am also grateful to the Saint Louis Priory School. It provided me with top notch computer and printing capabilities.

Without my family, I could not have finished this project. I thank my parents for providing me with the best education anyone could hope to have. In particular, I thank my mother for teaching me how to write, and I thank my father , Thomas Finan, for teaching me never to give up on anything I started. Finally, I am most grateful to my wife Debbie. Her unfailing belief in me keeps me going.